Media Track List

Audio and video can be found in the *Inside Listening and Speaking* Di
Go to www.insidelisteningandspeaking.com. Click on the Video Center
Click on the Audio Center ⬆ and choose to stream or download ⬇ the

UNIT 1

Listening	Listen	⬆	ILS_L0_U1_Listen
	Listen for Main Ideas	⬆	ILS_L0_U1_Listen
	Apply B	⬆	ILS_L0_U1_Listen
Speaking	Watch	▣	ILS_L0_U1_Watch
	Listen for Main Ideas	▣	ILS_L0_U1_Watch
	Apply A	▣	ILS_L0_U1_Watch
Pronunciation	Learn A	⬆	ILS_L0_U1_Pron_LearnA
	Learn B	⬆	ILS_L0_U1_Pron_LearnB
	Apply A	⬆	ILS_L0_U1_Pron_ApplyA
	Apply B	⬆	ILS_L0_U1_Pron_ApplyB

UNIT 2

Listening	Listen	⬆	ILS_L0_U2_Listen
	Listen for Main Ideas	⬆	ILS_L0_U2_Listen
	Apply A	⬆	ILS_L0_U2_Listen
Speaking	Watch	▣	ILS_L0_U2_Watch
	Listen for Main Ideas	▣	ILS_L0_U2_Watch
	Apply A	▣	ILS_L0_U2_Watch
	Apply B	⬆	ILS_L0_U2_Speak_ApplyB
Pronunciation	Learn A	⬆	ILS_L0_U2_Pron_LearnA
	Learn B	⬆	ILS_L0_U2_Pron_LearnB
	Learn C	⬆	ILS_L0_U2_Pron_LearnC
End of Unit Task	A	⬆	ILS_L0_U2_End
	B	⬆	ILS_L0_U2_End

UNIT 3

Listening	Watch	▣	ILS_L0_U3_Watch
	Listen for Main Ideas	▣	ILS_L0_U3_Watch
	Apply A	▣	ILS_L0_U3_Watch
Speaking	Listen	⬆	ILS_L0_U3_Listen
	Listen for Main Ideas	⬆	ILS_L0_U3_Listen
	Apply A	⬆	ILS_L0_U3_Speak_ApplyA
Pronunciation	Learn A	⬆	ILS_L0_U3_Pron_LearnA
	Learn B	⬆	ILS_L0_U3_Pron_LearnB
	Apply A	⬆	ILS_L0_U3_Pron_ApplyA
	Apply B	⬆	ILS_L0_U3_Pron_ApplyB
End of Unit Task	A	⬆	ILS_L0_U3_End
	B	⬆	ILS_L0_U3_End

UNIT 4

Listening	Listen	⬆	ILS_L0_U4_Listen
	Listen for Main Ideas	⬆	ILS_L0_U4_Listen
	Apply A	⬆	ILS_L0_U4_Note_ApplyA
	Apply B	⬆	ILS_L0_U4_Note_ApplyB
	Apply C	⬆	ILS_L0_U4_Note_ApplyC
Speaking	Watch	▣	ILS_L0_U4_Watch
	Listen for Main Ideas	▣	ILS_L0_U4_Watch
	Apply A	▣	ILS_L0_U4_Speak_ApplyA
	Apply B	▣	ILS_L0_U4_Watch
Pronunciation	Learn A	⬆	ILS_L0_U4_Pron_LearnA
	Learn B	⬆	ILS_L0_U4_Pron_LearnB
	Apply A	⬆	ILS_L0_U4_Pron_ApplyA

UNIT 5

Listening	Listen	⬆	ILS_L0_U5_Listen1
	Listen for Main Ideas	⬆	ILS_L0_U5_Listen1
	Apply B	⬆	ILS_L0_U5_Listen_ApplyB
Speaking	Listen	⬆	ILS_L0_U5_Listen2
	Listen for Main Ideas	⬆	ILS_L0_U5_Listen2
	Apply A	⬆	ILS_L0_U5_Listen2
	Apply B	⬆	ILS_L0_U5_Speak_ApplyB
	Apply C	⬆	ILS_L0_U5_Listen2
Pronunciation	Learn A	⬆	ILS_L0_U5_Pron_LearnA
	Learn B	⬆	ILS_L0_U5_Pron_LearnB
	Learn C	⬆	ILS_L0_U5_Pron_LearnC
	Apply A	⬆	ILS_L0_U5_Pron_ApplyA
	Apply B	⬆	ILS_L0_U5_Pron_ApplyB
End of Unit Task	A	⬆	ILS_L0_U5_End

UNIT 6

Listening	Listen	⬆	ILS_L0_U6_Listen
	Listen for Main Ideas	⬆	ILS_L0_U6_Listen
	Learn B	⬆	ILS_L0_U6_Listen
Speaking	Watch	▣	ILS_L0_U6_Watch
	Listen for Main Ideas	▣	ILS_L0_U6_Watch
	Apply A	▣	ILS_L0_U6_Watch
Pronunciation	Learn A	⬆	ILS_L0_U6_Pron_LearnA
	Learn B	⬆	ILS_L0_U6_Pron_LearnB
	Learn C	⬆	ILS_L0_U6_Pron_LearnC
	Learn D	⬆	ILS_L0_U6_Pron_LearnD
	Apply A	⬆	ILS_L0_U6_Pron_ApplyA
End of Unit Task	A	▣	ILS_L0_U6_Watch

UNIT 7

Listening	Listen	⬆	ILS_L0_U7_Listen
	Listen for Main Ideas	⬆	ILS_L0_U7_Listen
	Apply A	⬆	ILS_L0_U7_Listen
	Apply B	⬆	ILS_L0_U7_Listen
Speaking	Watch	▣	ILS_L0_U7_Watch
	Listen for Main Ideas	▣	ILS_L0_U7_Watch
	Apply A	▣	ILS_L0_U7_Watch
Pronunciation	Learn A	⬆	ILS_L0_U7_Pron_LearnA
	Learn B	⬆	ILS_L0_U7_Pron_LearnB
	Learn C	⬆	ILS_L0_U7_Pron_LearnC
	Apply A	⬆	ILS_L0_U7_Pron_ApplyA

UNIT 8

Listening	Watch	▣	ILS_L0_U8_Watch
	Listen for Main Ideas	▣	ILS_L0_U8_Watch
	Learn A	▣	ILS_L0_U8_Listen_LearnA
	Apply A	▣	ILS_L0_U8_Listen_ApplyA
	Apply B	▣	ILS_L0_U8_Listen_ApplyB
Speaking	Listen	⬆	ILS_L0_U8_Listen
	Listen for Main Ideas	⬆	ILS_L0_U8_Listen
	Apply A	⬆	ILS_L0_U8_Speak_ApplyA
Pronunciation	Learn A	⬆	ILS_L0_U8_Pron_LearnA
	Learn B	⬆	ILS_L0_U8_Pron_LearnB
	Learn C	⬆	ILS_L0_U8_Pron_LearnC
End of Unit Task	A	⬆	ILS_L0_U8_End
	B	⬆	ILS_L0_U8_End

UNIT 9

Listening	Watch	▣	ILS_L0_U9_Watch
	Listen for Main Ideas	▣	ILS_L0_U9_Watch
	Apply A	▣	ILS_L0_U9_Watch
	Apply B	▣	ILS_L0_U9_Watch
Speaking	Listen	⬆	ILS_L0_U9_Listen
	Listen for Main Ideas	⬆	ILS_L0_U9_Listen
	Apply A	⬆	ILS_L0_U9_Listen
Pronunciation	Learn A	⬆	ILS_L0_U9_Pron_LearnA
	Learn B	⬆	ILS_L0_U9_Pron_LearnB
	Learn C	⬆	ILS_L0_U9_Pron_LearnC
	Apply A	⬆	ILS_L0_U9_Pron_ApplyA
	Apply B	⬆	ILS_L0_U9_Pron_ApplyB

UNIT 10

Listening	Listen	⬆	ILS_L0_U10_Listen1
	Listen for Main Ideas	⬆	ILS_L0_U10_Listen1
	Apply A	⬆	ILS_L0_U10_Listen1
Speaking	Listen	⬆	ILS_L0_U10_Listen2
	Listen for Main Ideas	⬆	ILS_L0_U10_Listen2
	Apply A	⬆	ILS_L0_U10_Listen2
Pronunciation	Learn A	⬆	ILS_L0_U10_Pron_LearnA
	Learn B	⬆	ILS_L0_U10_Pron_LearnB
	Apply A	⬆	ILS_L0_U10_Pron_ApplyA

OXFORD
UNIVERSITY PRESS

198 Madison Avenue
New York, NY 10016 USA

Great Clarendon Street, Oxford, OX2 6DP, United Kingdom

Oxford University Press is a department of the University of Oxford.
It furthers the University's objective of excellence in research, scholarship,
and education by publishing worldwide. Oxford is a registered trade
mark of Oxford University Press in the UK and in certain other countries

© Oxford University Press 2016

The moral rights of the author have been asserted

First published in 2016

2020 2019 2018 2017 2016

10 9 8 7 6 5 4 3 2 1

No unauthorized photocopying

All rights reserved. No part of this publication may be reproduced, stored
in a retrieval system, or transmitted, in any form or by any means, without
the prior permission in writing of Oxford University Press, or as expressly
permitted by law, by licence or under terms agreed with the appropriate
reprographics rights organization. Enquiries concerning reproduction outside
the scope of the above should be sent to the ELT Rights Department, Oxford
University Press, at the address above

You must not circulate this work in any other form and you must impose
this same condition on any acquirer

Links to third party websites are provided by Oxford in good faith and for
information only. Oxford disclaims any responsibility for the materials
contained in any third party website referenced in this work

Adult Content Director: Stephanie Karras
Publisher: Sharon Sargent
Managing Editor: Tracey Gibbins
Senior Development Editor: Anna Norris
Associate Editor: Rachael Xerri
Head of Digital, Design, and Production: Bridget O'Lavin
Executive Art and Design Manager: Maj-Britt Hagsted
Content Production Manager: Julie Armstrong
Design Project Manager: Mary Chandler
Image Manager: Trisha Masterson

ISBN: 978 0 19 471904 9

Printed in China

This book is printed on paper from certified and well-managed sources

ACKNOWLEDGEMENTS

Illustration by: Infomen p. 19 (nurse, line graph, pie chart, eye chart,
organizational cart).

*We would also like to thank the following for permission to reproduce the following
photographs*: **Cover**, Brigitte Merle/Photononstop/Corbis; amanaimages/Corbis;
Franz-Marc Frei/Corbis; Nathan Benn/Corbis; Michael Prince/Corbis; Kamira/
Shutterstock; Eliks/Shutterstock; Frank Pali/age fotostock/SuperStock; pg. 1:
Interior, Alamy pp. 4 (Chinese man/Blend Images), 8 (illustration of hand/
David Marchal), 13 (map/Maxim Basinski), 40 (iPhone displaying Google
maps/Oleksiy Maksymenko Photography), 68 (hamburger/D. Hurst), 92
(photography exhibition/Guy Bell); Corbis UK Ltd. p. 52 (students in grass/
amanaimages); Getty Images pp. 20 (map and compass/John T. Wong), 56
(Wheelchair-bound college student/Pamela Moore), 61 (korean food/Iain
Bagwell), 64 (pub/Chris Laurens), 80 (Neon signs/Lonely Planet), 100 (San
Andreas Fault/Baron Wolman), 104 (Eruption of Kilauea Volcano/Jim Sugar);
masterfile.com p. 76 (Amsterdam/AWL Images); Oxford University Press p.
16 (couple with map/Radius Images); Redux Pictures Archive p. 88 (John
Bramblitt/Brandon Thibodeaux/The New York); Shutterstock pp. 1 (woman
smiling/mimagephotography), 25 (bee with flowers/Swapan Photography),
28 (Millennium Seed Bank/Tomasz Jasiewicz), 32 (Bees on honeycomb/Reluk),
37 (hand pressing social media icon/ra2studio), 44 (student/Vadim Ivanov),
49 (Modern Educational Facility/CreativeNature R.Zwerver), 73 (logotype
collection/Bloomua), 85 (Paints and brushes/Zadorozhnyi Viktor), 91 (heart
icon/Icon design), 91 (money bag icon/Blan-k), 91 (cutlery icon/Blan-k), 91 (bag
icon/Design Seed), 91 (recycle icon/vladis.studio), 97 (Earth's fault lines/Mopic),
109 (tool box/yevgeniy11), 112 (two Screw Drivers/Tei Sinthipsomboon), 116
(bicycle/AppleZoomZoom).

Acknowledgements

We would like to acknowledge the following individuals for their input during the development of the series:

Salam Affouneh
Higher Colleges of Technology
Abu Dhabi, U.A.E.

Kristin Bouton
Intensive English Institute
Illinois, U.S.A.

Nicole H. Carrasquel
Center for Multilingual Multicultural Studies
Florida, U.S.A.

Elaine Cockerham
Higher College of Technology
Muscat, Oman

Danielle Dilkes
CultureWorks English as a Second Language Inc.
Ontario, Canada

Susan Donaldson
Tacoma Community College
Washington, U.S.A

Penelope Doyle
Higher Colleges of Technology
Dubai, U.A.E.

Edward Roland Gray
Yonsei University
Seoul, South Korea

Melanie Golbert
Higher Colleges of Technology
Abu Dhabi, U.A.E.

Elise Harbin
Alabama Language Institute
Alabama, U.S.A.

Bill Hodges
University of Guelph
Ontario, Canada

David Daniel Howard
National Chiayi University
Chiayi

Leander Hughes
Saitama Daigaku
Saitama, Japan

James Ishler
Higher Colleges of Technology
Fujairah, U.A.E.

John Iveson
Sheridan College
Ontario, Canada

Alan Lanes
Higher Colleges of Technology
Dubai, U.A.E.

Corinne Marshall
Fanshawe College
Ontario, Canada

Christine Matta
College of DuPage
Illinois, U.S.A.

Beth Montag
University at Kearney
Nebraska, U.S.A.

Kevin Mueller
Tokyo International University
Saitama, Japan

Tracy Anne Munteanu
Higher Colleges of Technology
Fujairah, U.A.E.

Eileen O'Brien
Khalifa University of Science, Technology, and Research
Sharjah, U.A.E.

Jangyo Parsons
Kookmin University
Seoul, South Korea

John P. Racine
Dokkyo Daigaku
Soka City, Japan

Scott Rousseau
American University of Sharjah
Sharjah, U.A.E.

Jane Ryther
American River College
California, U.S.A

Kate Tindle
Zayed University
Dubai, U.A.E.

Melody Traylor
Higher Colleges of Technology
Fujairah, U.A.E.

John Vogels
Higher Colleges of Technology
Dubai, U.A.E.

Kelly Wharton
Fanshawe College
Ontario, Canada

Contents

The Inside Track to Academic Success

Student Books

For additional student resources, visit: www.insidelisteningandspeaking.com.

iTools for all levels

The *Inside Listening and Speaking* iTools component is for use with a projector or interactive whiteboard.

Resources for whole-class presentation

> **Book-on-screen** focuses class on teaching points and facilitates classroom management.

> **Audio and video** at point of use facilitates engaging, dynamic lessons.

Resources for assessment and preparation

> Customizable Unit, Mid-term, and Final Tests evaluate student progress.

> Complete Answer Keys are provided.

For additional instructor resources, visit:
www.oup.com/elt/teacher/insidelisteningandspeaking.

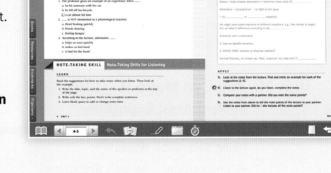

About *Inside Listening and Speaking*

Unit features

> **Explicit skills instruction** prepares students for academic listening

> **Authentic videos** from a variety of academic contexts engage and motivate students

> **Pronunciation instruction** ensures students are articulate, clear speakers

---

EARTH SCIENCE

UNIT 9

Dynamic Earth

In this unit, you will
> learn about tectonic plates and volcanoes.
> increase your understanding of the target academic words for this unit.

LISTENING AND SPEAKING SKILLS
> Key Terms and Definitions
> Asking for Clarification
> **PRONUNCIATION** Chunking

> Identifying the unit's goals focuses students on the **listening and speaking skills** and the academic topic.

Self-Assessment
Think about how well you know each target word, and check (✓) the appropriate column. I have...

TARGET WORDS	never seen this word before.	heard or seen the word but am not sure what it means.	heard or seen the word and understand what it means.	used the word confidently in *either* speaking or writing.
AWL				
🔑 appreciate				
🔑 energy				
🔑 predict				
🔑 previous				
🔑 remove				
🔑 role				
🔑 section				
🔑 series				

🔑 Oxford 3000™ keywords

> **Self-assessment** prepares students for the vocabulary in the audio and video activities.

The Academic Word List and the Oxford 3000

Based on a corpus of 4.3 million words, the **Academic Word List (AWL)** is the most principled and widely accepted list of academic words. Compiled by Averil Coxhead in 2000, it was informed by academic materials across the academic disciplines.

The **Oxford 3000™** have been carefully selected by a group of language experts and experienced teachers as the most important and useful words to learn in English. The Oxford 3000 are based on the American English section of the Oxford English Corpus.

> **Oxford 3000 and Academic Word List vocabulary** is integrated throughout the unit and practiced in context through audio and video resources.

Explicit Skills Instruction

Before You Listen

Read these questions. Discuss your answers in a small group.

1. Have you ever seen an active volcano? Where and when?
2. Can you name any well-known volcanoes? Which ones?
3. What kind of damage is caused by a volcanic eruption?

> **Discussion questions activate students' knowledge** and prepare them to listen.

Listen

Read the Listen for Main Ideas activity below. Go online to listen to an explanation of what happens when a volcano erupts.

Listen for Main Ideas

Number the topics 1–5 in the order that they are discussed. Compare your answers with a partner.

____ Predicting volcanoes

____ Tectonic plates

____ The effects of a volcanic eruption

____ The Ring of Fire

____ How volcanoes happen

> **Comprehension activities** help students understand the listening materials in preparation for academic skills instruction.

SPEAKING SKILL   Asking for Clarification

LEARN

When you don't understand something, or you miss an important piece of information in a lecture or a study group, you need to ask the speaker to clarify or repeat the information. Below are some expressions that you can use to ask for clarification.

Asking for clarification
May I ask a question?
(I'm sorry.) I (still) don't understand.
I didn't understand the part about …
Could you please repeat that?
Could you please explain that?
Could you give us an example?
Do you mean … ?

> **Listening and speaking skill instruction** is linked to the academic content. **Apply** sections give students the opportunity to practice the skills in context.

APPLY

A. Listen to the conversation again and circle the expressions in the box on page 104 that the students use to ask for clarification. Compare your answers with a partner.

B. Choose one of the descriptions A–C below. (<u>Do not</u> read the other descriptions.) Read the one you chose carefully. Make sure that you understand and can pronounce the underlined words. Use a dictionary if necessary.

> A: There are three kinds of volcanoes: <u>active</u>, <u>dormant</u>, and <u>extinct</u>. An active volcano erupts regularly. A dormant volcano has erupted in the past but is now quiet. An extinct volcano is unlikely to erupt again. There are around <u>1,500</u> active volcanoes in the world.

> B: When a volcano erupts, it sends <u>ash</u>, <u>gas</u>, and <u>magma</u> into the air. On the ground, a volcanic eruption can also cause <u>earthquakes</u>, <u>floods</u>, and <u>tsunamis</u>, and destroy the landscape for miles around.

> C: The world's largest active volcano is <u>Mauna Loa</u>, which is located in <u>Hawaii</u>. Mauna Loa is <u>13,677</u> feet above sea level. From its base below sea level to its peak, it is higher than Mount Everest.

High-Interest Media Content

About the Topic

Artists use shape and color to describe what they see. But what if an artist is blind? John Bramblitt is an unusual artist because he is blind. He uses touch to "see" his subjects. His paintings are very colorful and express a lot of emotion.

Audio and video including lectures, professional presentations, classroom discussions, and student presentations expose students to a **variety of academic contexts**.

Before You Watch

Read these questions. Discuss your answers in a small group.

1. Have you ever drawn or painted a picture? What are the steps in the process of making a painting?
2. Do you know any artists? Describe them. What qualities are important to be a good artist?
3. What would be some challenges for an artist who can't see?

Watch

Read the Listen for Main Ideas activity below. Go online to watch John Bramblitt talk about his work and experience as an artist who is blind.

High-interest, original academic video and authentic BBC content motivate students.

Listen for Main Ideas

Mark each sentence as *T* (true) or F (false). Work with a partner. Restate false sentences to make them correct.

_F_ 1. John Bramblitt has always been blind.

___ 2. He uses his fingers to feel the paint and mix colors.

___ 3. He met his wife before he was blind, so he knows what she looks like.

___ 4. He teaches children his techniques for painting.

___ 5. He is very positive about the future.

LISTENING SKILL Summarizing after You Listen

LEARN

Summarizing means restating the main points of what you hear in a few sentences. Summarizing can help you remember what you've heard and show that you've understood. Use these guidelines to make a summary after you listen.

1. Make notes.
2. Re-read your notes and choose the main points.
3. Write the main points in a paragraph. Don't include minor details.

Pronunciation Instruction

Pronunciation skill instruction is supported by audio resources to ensure students are articulate, clear speakers.

PRONUNCIATION SKILL   Chunking

LEARN

In Units 7 and 8, you learned that a chunk is a meaningful word or group of words in a sentence. There are many different examples of chunking in spoken speech. Chunks can have their own intonation, which is the rise and fall of speech.

When you list a series of items, each item is one chunk. Items can be single words or phrases. Pause (|) after each item. Use rising intonation after each item until the final item. Use falling intonation on the final item.

A. Go online to listen to the following sentences.

1. It runs along the ocean floor, | rises above the sea, | and cuts a sharp line.
2. It's an area that runs from New Zealand | through Indonesia, | Japan, | Alaska, | and down the west coast of North America.

When words are spelled out loud, the letters are usually chunked in groups of two, three, or four. Use rising intonation on each chunk except the last one, and insert a pause (|) after each item.

B. Go online to listen to the examples.

1. *Appreciate* is spelled A-P-P | R-E-C | I-A-T-E.
2. *Tectonic* is spelled T-E-C | T-O-N | I-C.

When long sets of numbers are said out loud, these are also usually chunked in groups of two, three, or four numbers. Use rising intonation on each chunk except the last one, and insert a pause (|) after each item.

C. Go online to listen to the examples.

1. My phone number is 617 | 555 | 0076.
2. The password is 899 | 25 | 66.

APPLY

A. Go online to listen to the sentences. Draw lines showing pauses. Then draw arrows showing the appropriate intonation above the items.

1. The lower plate becomes hot, | the rock melts, | and the melted rock is pushed up to the Earth's surface.
2. Tectonic plates carry entire continents, extend far under the sea, and meet at the plate boundary.
3. Scientists try to predict earthquakes, volcanoes, and other forces of nature.

Students **learn and apply** pronunciation skills in the context of the academic topic.

106   UNIT 9

UNIT 1

Mind and Body

In this unit, you will

> learn about emotions and how they affect the body.
> increase your understanding of the target academic words for this unit.

LISTENING AND SPEAKING SKILLS

> Note-Taking Skills for Listening
> Basic Presentation Skills
> **PRONUNCIATION** Syllables and Word Stress

Self-Assessment

Think about how well you know each target word, and check (✓) the appropriate column. I have…

TARGET WORDS	never seen this word before.	heard or seen the word but am not sure what it means.	heard or seen the word and understand what it means.	used the word confidently in *either* speaking or writing.
AWL				
🔑 author				
🔑 final				
🔑 illustrate				
🔑 individual				
🔑 label				
🔑 physical				
🔑 publish				
🔑 text				

🔑 Oxford 3000™ keywords

Vocabulary Activities

A. Use the following target words, or forms of them, to complete the paragraph. One word is used twice.

finally	individual	label	physical

Do you sweat when you feel nervous? For example, when you have to speak in public, does your heart beat fast and do your hands shake? These are examples of ___physical___ reactions to the emotion of fear. Each _____
(1. bodily)   (2. person)

will be more or less nervous in different situations, but public speaking is a very common fear. Some people say that you can control these reactions if you

_____ the emotion differently. For example, if you tell yourself that you
(3. name)

are excited rather than scared, your _____ reaction might be different.
(4. bodily)

_____, remember that almost everyone feels the same as you.
(5. in the end)

B. Complete the Word Form Chart below with the correct forms of the target words. Use a dictionary to check your answers.

final	finals	individually	labeled	physical
finally	individual	label	labeling	physically
finalize				

Word Form Chart

Noun	Verb	Adjective	Adverb
final			

The word *physical* is related to the body. It can be used as an adjective or an adverb.

> *Physical activity is good for children. (adjective)*
>
> *A marathon runner is very physically fit. (adverb)*

CORPUS

C. Ask and answer the following questions with a partner.

1. How important is physical education in school? *Physical education is very important. Too many children are unhealthy and overweight these days.*

2. What is your favorite physical activity?

3. Why do people need physical therapy?

4. Do you know anyone who is very physically fit?

The word *label* means a piece of paper, etc., on an object that gives information about it. It can be a noun or a verb.

*There is a **label** on the folder that says what the topic is. (noun)*

*Please **label** the folder so we know what is in it. (verb)*

A person or thing can also be *labeled* when he / she / it is described in a particular way, especially unfairly.

*Because she kept to herself, Anna was **labeled** as stuck-up.*

 CORPUS

D. Work in pairs. Say which item usually has a label. For the items that have a label, say what it shows.

1. a can of soup *The label on a can of soup says what is in the soup.*

2. a pen *A pen doesn't usually have a label.*

3. an envelope

4. a table

5. a pair of jeans

E. Collocations are words that often go together. For example, *education* is often used with *physical*, as in "physical education." Create collocations with the target words from this unit and then ask and answer the questions.

1. a(an) average / powerful / single / talented / unique ___*individual*___

2. a clothing / designer / mailing _____

3. a _____ chapter / decision / exam

4. Who do you know that is a **unique individual**? _____

5. Do you wear clothes with **designer labels**? _____

About the Topic

Physiology is the study of how our bodies function. For example, when we feel a strong emotion, such as fear or excitement, our bodies react in a certain way: our hearts beat faster and our hands shake. This response is caused by the hormone *adrenalin*.

Before You Listen

Read these questions. Discuss your answers in a small group.

1. What are some different emotions or feelings people have?

2. How does your body react to strong emotions like fear or sadness?

3. Why do you think we react this way?

Listen

Read the Listen for Main Ideas activity below. Go online to listen to a professor lecture about how people react physically to emotions.

Listen for Main Ideas

Circle the best answer to complete each sentence. Then compare your answers with a partner.

1. The professor gives an example of an experience when ___.

    a. he hit someone with his car

    b. he fell off his bicycle

    c. a car almost hit him

2. ___ is NOT mentioned as a physiological reaction.

    a. Heart beating quickly

    b. Hands shaking

    c. Feeling hungry

3. According to the lecture, adrenaline ___.

    a. helps us react quickly

    b. makes us feel tired

    c. is bad for the heart

NOTE-TAKING SKILL   Note-Taking Skills for Listening

LEARN

Read the suggestions for how to take notes when you listen. Then look at the example.

1. Write the date, topic, and the name of the speaker or professor at the top of the page.

2. Write only the key points. Don't write complete sentences.

3. Leave blank space to add or change notes later.

4. Use numbering (1, 2, 3 …), bullet points (•), and / or arrows (→) to organize information.
5. <u>Underline</u>, highlight, or use CAPITAL LETTERS for important points.
6. Use abbreviations when you can. Here are some common abbreviations:

=	equals, is the same as	*adrenaline = hormone*
e.g.	for example,	*physiological reactions, e.g., heart beating*
etc.	et cetera, and so on	*emotions (fear, anger, etc.)*

The Physiology of Emotions   *Prof. Wheeler*   *Jan. 28*

Physiology of Emotions = what happens to bodies when <u>feel emotions</u> (e.g., fear, anger, etc.)

strong emotion = physiological reactions, e.g., almost hit by car:

heart beating faster, (1) _____, (2) _____

Other examples: sweat, breathe quickly, (3) _____, cry.

Stress = body creates adrenaline (= hormone) helps body (4) _____

Adrenaline = increased air → to fight or run away

= (5) _____ or _____ response

We might have same reactions in different situations, e.g., fear similar to anger. But we label it differently according to (6) _____.

Scientists don't understand

1. how we identify emotions.

2. WHICH FIRST: emotion or physical reaction?

Several theories, no answer yet. Phys. response very real and (7) _____.

APPLY

A. Look at the notes from the lecture. Find and circle an example for each of the suggestions (1–6).

B. Listen to the lecture again. As you listen, complete the notes.

C. Compare your notes with a partner. Did you note the same points?

D. Use the notes from above to tell the main points of the lecture to your partner. Listen to your partner. Did he / she include all the main points?

Vocabulary Activities

A. Read the book review below. For each sentence, cross out the word in parentheses with a different meaning from the other two choices. Compare your answers with a partner.

1. *Introduction to Physiology* was (*printed / published / written*) in 2011 by McPherson Press.

2. The (*author / publisher / writer*) is Carol Kerr, who is a professor of biology at the University of Atlanta.

3. The book contains hundreds of (*examples / illustrations / pictures*) of the human body.

4. The parts of the body are clearly (*identified / labeled / formed*).

5. The (*author / text / writing*) is simple and clear, so it is easy to understand.

6. The (*final / first / last*) chapter contains a useful summary of the main points of the book.

Word Form Chart		
Noun	**Verb**	**Adjective**
illustration	illustrate	illustrated
publisher	publish	published
text	text	_____

B. Using the target words in the Word Form Chart, complete the sentences. Be sure to use the correct form and tense of each word.

1. The ___*publisher*___ of *Inside Listening and Speaking* is Oxford University Press.

2. We have to use this book in our physiology class. It's a required _____ .

3. Children's books usually have a lot of _____ .

4. The professor liked my paper very much. He wants to _____ it in a student magazine.

5. I'm going to use an example to _____ my point.

6. It's often cheaper to send a _____ than to make a phone call.

The word *illustrate* means to add pictures or diagrams to a book. It is often used in the passive.

*The book is beautifully **illustrated**.*

To *illustrate* also means to explain something by using pictures, examples, or diagrams.

*This photograph **illustrates** the point I was making.*

CORPUS

C. Choose a method on the left that could illustrate an idea on the right. Discuss your ideas with a partner.

*A diagram could **illustrate** how blood moves around the body.*

1. a diagram	why physical exercise is important
2. a short video	how blood moves around the body
3. some statistics	types of healthy food
4. some examples	how to lift a piano safely

To *publish* is to produce a book, magazine, or website and make it public.

*The report will be **published** on the Internet.*

It can also mean to have your work printed in a book or a magazine.

*Doctor Garcia has **published** several papers online.*

The company that publishes books and magazines is a *publisher*.

CORPUS

D. Look at the book citations. Describe each book, using the words below.

author(s)	illustrated	published	publisher	text

*The first text is called Nutrition for Sport and Exercise. The **authors** are Marie Dunford and Andrew Doyle. The book was **published** in 2011. The **publisher** was Wadsworth Publishing.*

1. Marie Dunford and Andrew Doyle, *Nutrition for Sport and Exercise.* Wadsworth Publishing, 2011.
2. Johannes Fox, *An Illustrated Guide to Human Anatomy.* Smith and Carter Publications, 2010.
3. Claire Wong, *Fitness for Everyone.* Popular Press, 2002.
4. Brian Garcia, *Strength Training for All (Illustrated).* Schoolhouse Publishing, 2001.

About the Topic

One of the most popular textbooks in the world is *Gray's Anatomy*. It is a medical reference book that has been used by doctors, surgeons, and medical students for over 150 years.

Before You Watch

Read these questions. Discuss your answers in a small group.

1. Anatomy is the study of the different parts of the body. Who has to study anatomy?

2. Do you think anatomy is easy to learn? Why or why not?

3. How can a textbook help students to learn anatomy?

Watch

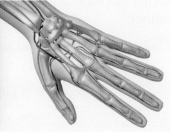

Read the Listen for Main Ideas activity below. Go online to watch a student give a presentation about the creation of *Gray's Anatomy*.

Listen for Main Ideas

Mark each sentence as *T* (true) or *F* (false). Work with a partner. Restate false sentences to make them correct.

__T__ 1. Henry Gray was a surgeon who wrote a textbook.

____ 2. Henry Vandyke Carter was very good at drawing.

____ 3. The two men worked together to create the book.

____ 4. Carter wrote part of the text of the book.

____ 5. Gray and Carter got equal credit and equal money for the book.

PRESENTATION SKILL   Basic Presentation Skills

LEARN

Good presenters appear calm and confident. They prepare notes to refer to, but do not read directly from their notes. Use the suggestions in the box to help you.

Basic Presentation Skills
1. Stand up straight, with your shoulders back. Relax.
2. As you speak, look at the audience. Don't look at only one person. Look at people around the room.
3. Speak a little more slowly than usual. Pause often.
4. Use your voice to keep people's attention. For example, speak more loudly and clearly to stress important points.
5. Use notes, but don't write every word. Just write the main points.
6. In your notes, underline or highlight key words.

APPLY

A. Watch the presentation again. Which of the suggestions on page 8 does the speaker follow?

B. Prepare a short presentation (one to two minutes) about yourself. Use the prompts below to make notes. Underline the important words and phrases in your notes.

- My name:
- Where I was born, and where my family lives now:
- My family:
- Where I went to school and what I studied and / or where I work:
- What I like to do in my free time:

C. Work with a partner. Practice your presentation. Listen to your partner's presentation. Use the checklist below to make notes about your partner's presentation. Then compare and discuss your checklists.

Name: _____ Topic: _____

Did the speaker …

1. stand up straight and appear relaxed?
2. look at people in different parts of the room?
3. speak slowly enough to be understood, with pauses?
4. use notes without reading from them?
5. pronounce key words clearly?

D. Give your presentation to your classmates.

PRONUNCIATION SKILL Syllables and Word Stress

LEARN

Each part of a word with a vowel sound is called a syllable. There may be a consonant before, after, or before and after this vowel sound.

A. Go online to listen to the words and notice how some words have only one syllable and some words have two or more. Each syllable is separated by the • symbol.

au • thor	la • bel
il • lu • strate	text

A syllable can be stressed or unstressed. The stressed syllable in a word is pronounced longer, stronger, and higher than the other syllables in the word. The vowel sound is also lengthened.

B. Go online to listen to the words. Look at the following chart, which shows in pink which vowel sound is lengthened.

fi • nal	**phy** • si • cal
in • di • **vid** • u • al	**pu** • blish

APPLY

A. Go online to listen to the words. In the right column, write how many syllables you hear in each word.

1. description	3
2. stomach	
3. information	
4. heart	
5. physiology	
6. situation	

B. Go online to listen to the words. Circle the syllable that is stressed. The vowel sound will be lengthened.

1. e • (mo) • tion
2. re • sponse
3. com • pli • ca • ted
4. theo • ry

5. sci • en • tist
6. a • na • to • my
7. med • ic • al
8. pic • ture

C. Say the words in activities A and B. Stress the correct syllable and lengthen its vowel sound.

D. With a partner, find an online article about keeping the body healthy. Make a list of new words or words you've learned recently. Also use the words from activities A and B on page 10. Use each word in a sentence. Stress the correct syllable and lengthen its vowel sound. Use a dictionary or ask a native speaker if you have trouble determining which syllable to stress.

> Phy • si • cal. She had a **physical** reaction to the stressful situation.
>
> Sto • mach. My **stomach** hurts when I get nervous.

End of Unit Task

In this unit, you learned how to take notes while listening to a lecture. You also learned some strategies for giving an oral presentation. Review these skills by preparing and giving a short presentation to the class, and by taking notes on your classmates' presentations.

A. Prepare a one- to two-minute presentation about an activity that you enjoy doing. First, make some notes to answer the questions below. Underline the important words and phrases in your notes.

1. What is the activity?
2. How long have you been interested in it?
3. How often do you do it?
4. Where and when do you do it?
5. Do you do it alone or with other people?
6. Why do you enjoy it?

B. Practice your presentation with a partner. Use the suggestions in the box. Then listen to your partner's presentation and take notes.

1. Stand up straight, with your shoulders back. Relax.

2. As you speak, look at the audience. Don't look at only one person. Look at people around the room.

3. Speak a little more slowly than usual. Pause often.

4. Use your voice to keep people's attention. For example, speak more loudly and clearly to stress important points.

5. Use notes, but don't write every word. Just write the main points.

6. In your notes, underline or highlight key words.

C. Compare your notes with your partner. Did you write down the correct information? Give your partner feedback on how he / she can improve the presentation. Practice again if necessary.

D. Give your presentation again to the whole class. As you listen to the other presentations, take notes.

E. Complete the checklist below for one or more of your classmates.

Name: _____ Topic: _____

Did the speaker ...

1. stand up straight and appear relaxed?
2. look at people in different parts of the room?
3. speak slowly enough to be understood, with pauses?
4. use notes without reading from them?
5. pronounce key words clearly?

F. Give your classmate(s) feedback on their presentations.

Self-Assessment		
Yes	**No**	
☐	☐	I successfully took notes on my classmates' presentations.
☐	☐	I successfully prepared and used notes for my own presentation.
☐	☐	I gave a clear oral presentation about an activity that I enjoy.
☐	☐	I can understand syllables and word stress.
☐	☐	I can correctly use the target vocabulary words from the unit.

Discussion Questions

With a partner or in a small group, discuss the following questions.

1. Can you name some situations in which people have strong physiological reactions?
2. Can you give an example of a well-known book or publication that you enjoyed reading?
3. In your free time, do you prefer to do individual or group activities?

UNIT 2

Finding Your Way

In this unit, you will

> learn about geography and our sense of direction.
> increase your understanding of the target academic words for this unit.

LISTENING AND SPEAKING SKILLS

> Identifying Main Ideas
> Greeting and Leave-Taking
> **PRONUNCIATION** Intonation

Self-Assessment

Think about how well you know each target word, and check (✓) the appropriate column. I have…

TARGET WORDS	never seen this word before.	heard or seen the word but am not sure what it means.	heard or seen the word and understand what it means.	used the word confidently in *either* speaking or writing.
AWL				
🔑 accurate				
🔑 assist				
🔑 chapter				
🔑 chart				
🔑 device				
🔑 error				
🔑 feature				
🔑 tradition				

🔑 Oxford 3000™ keywords

Vocabulary Activities

A. Use the target words from the box to complete the paragraph. Be sure to use the correct form of each word. One word is used twice.

accurate	assist	error	feature

Our new GPS has many useful ___features___. The new system is
(1. important parts)

even more _____ than before. You'll find your way easily and
(2. exact)

with fewer _____ than those found in other electronic systems.
(3. mistakes)

Come to our store and one of our technicians will answer your questions

and _____ you. When you learn more about all the amazing
(4. help)

_____ of this system, you'll never leave home without it again!
(5. aspects)

B. *Feature* has multiple meanings. Match the dictionary definitions on the left with the example sentences on the right.

feature (noun)

Definitions

_b_ 1. an important or noticeable part of something

___ 2. a part of someone's face

___ 3. an article or TV program about someone or something

___ 4. the main movie in a theater

Example Sentences

a. This week's feature film is *Mission Impossible.*

b. The most important feature of the landscape is the lake.

c. There's a special feature on education in the newspaper today.

d. Her eyes are her best feature.

To *assist* someone is to help them.

> *The witnesses **assisted** the police with the investigation.*

The noun is *assistance*. It is usually used in formal contexts.

> *Is there a problem? May I be of **assistance**?*

> *Students may request financial **assistance** by completing this form.*

An *assistant* is someone who helps or supports someone. *Assistant* is often used before a noun or after an adjective.

> *We can't finish all of the work, so we need to hire a competent **assistant**.*

> *We have a new **assistant** manager at work.*

CORPUS

C. Complete the sentences with *assistant(s)* or *assistance*.

1. I don't go to that store. The sales __*assistants*__ are not very helpful.

2. My computer is having problems. I need technical _____.

3. A teaching _____ helps the professor with the class.

4. The government is giving economic _____ to developing countries.

5. The director of a movie usually has several _____ directors.

6. The manager is not here today. Would you like to speak to the _____ manager?

D. Discuss with a partner what kind of assistance each person gives.

1. a teaching assistant (TA) *A teaching assistant helps the teacher in a class.*
2. a sales assistant
3. an assistant coach
4. a research assistant
5. a dental assistant

Accurate is an adjective that means "correct and true; done in an exact way." The negative form is *inaccurate*.

> *That clock is **accurate**. It always shows the correct time.*

> *This report is **inaccurate**. It needs to be corrected.*

An *error* is a noun and is a more formal word for "a mistake."

> *There are many **errors** in the report.*

 CORPUS

E. Work with a partner. Discuss which of these items need to be accurate and why. Then say what happens if it is inaccurate or there is an error.

1. a map *A map needs to be accurate. If there is an error, you'll probably get lost.*
2. a description of a place in a novel
3. a bus or train schedule
4. a news story online or in a newspaper
5. a web page address
6. a children's story
7. a recipe

F. Work in a small group. Describe the main feature(s) of each of the following.

1. the landscape in your area *The main feature of the landscape in my area is the mountains.*
2. the climate in your area
3. a luxury car
4. a building that you know
5. a successful business
6. a person's face
7. a smartphone

About the Topic

The use of electronic systems is changing the way people navigate, or find their way from one place to another. Global Positioning Systems, known as GPS, are replacing paper maps. But GPS devices are not perfect. Both paper maps and GPS devices are useful tools for navigation.

Before You Listen

Read these questions. Discuss your answers in a small group.

1. Do you feel you have a good sense of direction? Why or why not?
2. How often do you use electronic systems like a GPS to find your way around?
3. What are some of the differences between using GPS and using a map?

Listen

Read the Listen for Main Ideas activity below. Go online to listen to a podcast of a radio show about science. The presenters discuss our sense of direction, and the things we use to help us find the way from one place to another.

Listen for Main Ideas

Mark each sentence as *T* (true) or *F* (false). Work with a partner. Restate false sentences to make them correct.

_T_ 1. People were probably better at finding their way in the past.

____ 2. A GPS isn't always useful because it doesn't show a large area.

____ 3. A study in Japan found that paper maps and a GPS were equal in helping people find their way.

____ 4. People who are good at finding their way probably notice details.

____ 5. The speaker gives an example of using a river to find his way.

Identifying Main Ideas

LEARN

When you listen, and when you take notes, you need to be able to identify the main points that the speaker is making. Those points are what the speaker wants you to learn or understand as you listen. Often, the main points are mentioned first and then followed by explanations or examples.

Look at a paragraph from the podcast. There are two main ideas in this section. One is underlined. Underline the other main idea in this section. Compare your answer with a partner.

> *Good morning. Welcome to Science World. <u>Today we're talking about direction</u>. Some people never get lost, while others need a GPS just to find their way to the store! It seems that humans were better at navigation in the past. Ancient explorers traveled thousands of miles across the oceans and found new lands.*

APPLY

A. **Listen to the audio again. As you listen, check (✓) the four main points that the speakers make.**

✓ 1. People were better at finding their way in the past.

___ 2. A lot of people have difficulty reading maps.

___ 3. Paper maps can be more useful than a GPS.

___ 4. A GPS doesn't show the features of the landscape.

___ 5. Many people get lost when using a GPS.

___ 6. People who notice details are better at finding their way.

___ 7. The man got lost when he was going to his friend's house.

B. **Work with a partner. Take turns summarizing the main points of the radio podcast. For each main point, add one detail or example that you remember.**

Vocabulary Activities

A. Read the following description of an improvement in medical care. Cross out the word in parentheses with a different meaning from the other two choices. Use a dictionary to help you understand new words. Compare answers with a partner.

1. MedTrack is a (~~computer~~ / *device* / *machine*) that helps keep track of patients' medications in a hospital.

2. (*Traditionally* / *Unfortunately* / *Usually*), nurses give medication to a patient and then make a note of the medication on a (*chart* / *form* / *textbook*).

3. But this system is often (*inaccurate* / *inexact* / *unpopular*), and nurses make (*errors* / *medications* / *mistakes*).

4. The new (*device* / *paper* / *tool*) should (*assist* / *help* / *involve*) medical staff in (*charting* / *forgetting* / *tracking*) a patient's medications more (*accurately* / *quickly* / *exactly*).

B. A *chapter* is a part of a book. Look at the chapter titles for a book about navigation. Work with a partner to answer the questions.

Chapter 1: Introduction to Navigation
Chapter 2: Using Maps
Chapter 3: Using a Compass
Chapter 4: Using Features of the Landscape to Navigate
Chapter 5: How to Use a GPS
Chapter 6: If You Are Lost

1. Where can you find information about maps? *Chapter 2*

2. Where is information about using a GPS?

3. Where can you learn about landscape features?

4. Which chapter explains what to do if you are lost?

5. Where is the introduction?

Word Form Chart			
Noun	**Verb**	**Adjective**	**Adverb**
tradition	_____	traditional non-traditional	traditionally

C. Using the target words in the Word Form Chart, complete these sentences. Be sure to use the correct form of each word.

1. _*Traditionally*_ , explorers used stars to help them navigate.

2. Does your family have any _____ to celebrate holidays?

3. The children wore _____ clothing for the celebration.

4. If you work from home, you may have a _____ job.

D. Work with a partner. Choose one of the items below. Write a description sentence using *device*. See if your partner can identify the item described.

> *A: It's an electronic **device** you use to find your way.*
> *B: A GPS.*

a can opener	a GPS	an iron	a microwave
a flash drive	a hair dryer	a metal detector	a computer mouse

A *chart* is a page that shows information in the form of a diagram, list, etc. It can also be a map of the ocean or of the sky.

> *The **chart** shows the company's profits over the last three years.*
>
> *Sailors use **charts** to navigate from one port to the next.*

Different kinds of charts are used to show different kinds of information.

CORPUS

E. Work with a partner. Say which person might use each kind of chart shown and explain why. See if you can add other examples of people and charts they use.

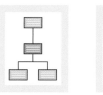

1. an eye doctor *An eye doctor would use an eye chart to test people's eyes.*
2. a doctor or nurse
3. a family making a budget
4. a business person planning a project

A *tradition* is a custom or belief that has been continued from the past.

> *It is a **tradition** in western countries for the bride to wear a white dress at a wedding.*

The adjective is *traditional*.

> *In many countries it is **traditional** to shake hands when you meet someone new.*

The adverb is *traditionally*.

> ***Traditionally**, a Thanksgiving turkey is cooked for several hours.*

CORPUS

F. Work in small groups. Discuss the questions.

1. What are some traditions that your family has?
2. What is a traditional food from your country?
3. What is your country's traditional clothing? Describe it. When do you wear it?
4. What are some holidays that are traditionally celebrated in your country? How do you celebrate them?

About the Topic

In the past, explorers and sailors used different navigational tools than pilots and navigators use today. Sometimes they relied on their observations of the winds, waves, and stars. As they traveled, they created their own maps.

Before You Watch

Read these questions. Discuss your answers in a small group.

1. What explorers can you name?
2. How did they find their way?
3. What kinds of tools did people use for navigation in the past?

Watch

Read the Listen for Main Ideas activity below. Go online to watch three students discuss their homework assignment before class.

Listen for Main Ideas

Listen to the conversation and look at the chapter titles below. Number the chapters 1–3 in the order they are discussed by the students.

Chapter Title	Page
____ Early Cartography and the First Mapmakers	.63
____ Early Navigational Tools and Devices	.75
____ Celestial Navigation: Using the Stars	.84

SPEAKING SKILL   Greeting and Leave-Taking

LEARN

The chart below shows some common ways to greet people and to say goodbye. Note that some expressions are more formal than others. Usually, very informal expressions are used with people that you know well. Neutral expressions can be used in most situations.

	Greeting	Leave-taking
Very informal	What's up?	Got to go.
Informal	Hi. / Hello. How are you doing? How's it going?	I've got to go. / I have to go. See you.

Neutral	Hello. How are you?	See you (later / tomorrow / next week). Bye.
More formal	Good morning. / Good afternoon. / Good evening.	Goodbye. I'll see you (later / tomorrow / next week).
Leaving for a short time (for example, to take a phone call)		Excuse me. I'll be right back.

APPLY

A. Go online to watch the video, and listen to the conversation again. Circle the expressions in the chart that you hear in the conversation.

B. Work with a partner. Read the conversations below. Discuss and note possible expressions for each blank. Listen and check your answers.

1. A: Good morning. _____?
   B: I'm fine, thank you.

2. A: Hi! _____?
   B: Great! How about you?
   A: Not bad.

3. A: Goodbye.
   B: Goodbye. _____ .

4. A: _____ . _____ .
   B: OK, yeah. _____ .

C. Work in pairs. Make conversations for the following situations. Try to continue each conversation beyond one exchange.

1. You are two students greeting one another before class. You know one another from previous classes.

    A: Hi, Ricardo. How's it going?
    B: Great! How are you?
    A: Oh, I'm fine. Hey, did you do the homework? I have a question about it.
    B: Yes, I did. What do you need to know?

2. You are a student. You meet your professor from last semester on campus.

3. You are two students greeting one another on the first day of class. You do not know one another.

4. You are two students having lunch together. One needs to step outside to take a phone call.

5. You are saying goodbye to your friend after class.

6. You are saying goodbye to your professor after class.

D. With a partner, role-play one of the above conversations in front of the class.

LEARN

Intonation is the rise and fall of your voice when you speak. Intonation tells you if someone is making a statement or asking a question, and what kind of question they are asking.

A. Your voice goes down, or falls, at the end of a statement. Go online to listen to the sentences. Notice the arrows that show falling intonation.

1. We use maps to navigate.
2. I get lost easily.
3. My GPS device is broken.

B. Your voice also goes down at the end of a question that uses a *wh-* word. Go online to listen to the sentences. Notice the arrows that show falling intonation.

1. How do we get there?
2. What is the address?
3. Who gave you those directions?

C. Your voice goes up, or rises, at the end of a yes / no question. Go online to listen to the sentences. Notice the arrows that show rising intonation.

1. Can you take me there?
2. Does the application have a directions feature?
3. Are they on their way?

APPLY

A. Say the sentences in activities A, B, and C above. Use the correct rising or falling intonation.

B. Make a list of three characteristics that the other students in your class might have: for example, "has a car," "likes to read," or "knows how to play an instrument." Ask your classmates if they have any of these characteristics, and get more information to learn more about them. Use the correct intonation.

A: Do you know how to play an instrument?

B: Yes, I do.

A: What instrument do you know how to play?

C. With a partner, ask for and give directions to a location at your school. Your partner answers with a place that is nearby. You can ask for more information using *wh-* words. Use the phrases in the box below. Use the correct rising or falling intonation.

> A: Do you know how to get to the cafeteria?
>
> B: Yes, I do. It's in the same building as the library.
>
> A: Where should I park my car if I go?

Do you know where … is?	What is close to it?
Can you tell me where … is?	It is near / across the street from / next door to …

End of Unit Task

In this unit, you learned about geography and our sense of direction. You listened for main ideas in a lecture. You also learned and practiced different ways of greeting and leave-taking. You will practice these skills in the following tasks.

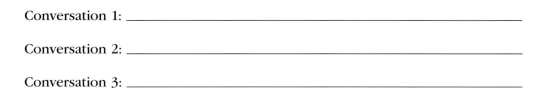 **A.** Go online and listen to three conversations on campus. What is the main idea of each conversation? Compare your answers in small groups.

Conversation 1: _____

Conversation 2: _____

Conversation 3: _____

B. Listen again. Circle the greeting and leave-taking expressions you hear. Compare your answers with a partner.

	Greeting	Leave-taking
Very informal	What's up?	Got to go.
Informal	Hi. / Hello. How are you doing? How's it going?	I've got to go. / I have to go. See you.
Neutral	Hello. How are you?	See you (later / tomorrow / next week). Bye.
More formal	Good morning. / Good afternoon. / Good evening.	Goodbye. I'll see you (later / tomorrow / next week).
Leaving for a short time (for example, to take a phone call)		Excuse me. I'll be right back.

C. Work with a partner. Choose one or more of the situations and make up conversations. Include greeting and leave-taking expressions.

1. A: You are at the campus library. You want to know how late the library will be open this weekend.

   B: You work at the campus library, but this is your first day. When someone asks for information, you need to check with your supervisor.

2. A: You are having problems with a paper for your history class. You need to ask your professor for help. You see your professor in the hallway.

   B: You are a professor. You have a class that starts in ten minutes. Your open office hour is Wednesday at 9 a.m.

3. A: You are in the cafeteria and see a classmate that you haven't seen for a long time. Greet him / her and chat for a few minutes.

   B: You haven't seen your friend since last semester, so you're happy to see him / her again. As you are talking, your cell phone rings. It's an important call.

D. Work in groups. Take turns and role-play the conversations above. What is the main idea of each one? Which greeting and leave-taking expressions are used?

Self-Assessment		
Yes	**No**	
☐	☐	I was able to identify the main ideas in the conversations.
☐	☐	I successfully identified greeting and leave-taking expressions in the conversations.
☐	☐	My partner and I successfully practiced greeting and leave-taking expressions.
☐	☐	I understand intonation in statements and questions.
☐	☐	I can correctly use the target vocabulary words from the unit.

Discussion Questions

With a partner or in a small group, discuss the following questions.

1. How do you usually find your way to a place you haven't been to?

2. In your opinion, is it easier to follow a map or a GPS device?

3. Have you ever been lost? If so, what did you do to find your way?

UNIT 3

The Life of Plants

In this unit, you will

> learn about seed and bee conservation.
> increase your understanding of the target academic words for this unit.

LISTENING AND SPEAKING SKILLS

> Understanding Spoken Numbers
> Considering Audience for a Presentation
> **PRONUNCIATION** Reduced Question Forms

Self-Assessment

Think about how well you know each target word, and check (✓) the appropriate column. I have…

TARGET WORDS	never seen this word before.	heard or seen the word but am not sure what it means.	heard or seen the word and understand what it means.	used the word confidently in *either* speaking or writing.
AWL				
🔑 expert				
🔑 grade				
🔑 initial				
🔑 issue				
🔑 partner				
🔑 research				
🔑 resource				
🔑 team				

🔑 Oxford 3000™ keywords

Vocabulary Activities

A. Read the paragraph. For each sentence, cross out the word in parentheses with a different meaning from the other two. Use a dictionary to help you understand new words. Compare answers with a partner.

They are starting a new project at my university to 1. (*study / grow / research*) plants. I would like to work on the project, but I'm not sure I have enough 2. (*books / knowledge / expertise*) yet. The university has a 3. (*partnership / collaboration / paper*) with another university for the project. People from both places will work together as 4. (*a team / one person / a group*) on the project. The main 5. (*researcher / scientist / boss*) is a professor from my university. Everyone likes her. She has managed many projects 6. (*well / badly / expertly*).

B. Work with a partner. Look at the underlined words in each sentence. Write *N* if the word is a noun, and *V* if the word is a verb.

_V_ 1. The students will <u>team</u> up for the project.

___ 2. The students will work together as a <u>team</u> on the project.

___ 3. They will <u>research</u> the topic for class.

___ 4. They will do <u>research</u> on the topic for class.

___ 5. The students will work with a <u>partner</u> on the project.

___ 6. The students will <u>partner</u> with a classmate on the project.

C. Check (✓) which of these people perform *research*. Compare answers with a partner. Can you think of other people who perform *research*?

_✓_ 1. a scientist

___ 2. a musician

___ 3. a writer

___ 4. a bus driver

___ 5. a student

___ 6. a medical doctor

___ 7. a waiter

D. Do these people work with a partner or on a team? Can any activities be done with either a partner or a team? Compare your answers with a partner.

1. a dancer *A dancer can dance alone or with a partner.*
2. a soccer player
3. someone who wants to start a business
4. a scientist who wants to do research
5. a basketball player
6. a group of people at work who need to complete a project
7. a tennis player

E. Work with a partner. Discuss what each person has to be an expert in or on.

1. a car mechanic *A car mechanic has to be an expert on how a car works. He or she should also have expertise in different types of cars.*
2. a medical doctor
3. a professional athlete
4. an artist
5. a writer
6. a teacher
7. a plant scientist

F. Match words from column A to words they go with from column B. The words in column B can be used more than once. Use a dictionary to help you. Then write an example sentence for each pair. Compare your answers with a partner.

A	B
academic	partner
business	partnership
market	research
scientific	team
winning	

scientific research: The university does important scientific research.

About the Topic

Many plant species around the world are endangered; some have become extinct. Scientists are working to conserve plants by collecting and saving seeds. Kew Garden's Millennium Seed Bank is one example of this kind of work.

Before You Watch

Read these questions. Discuss your answers in a small group.

1. Have you ever grown or had a plant? Where did you get the seeds?
2. In what ways are plants important to humans?
3. What do you think a seed bank is?

Watch

Read the Listen for Main Ideas activity below. Go online to watch how Kew Garden's Millennium Seed Bank is working to save seeds from around the world.

Listen for Main Ideas

Mark each sentence as *T* (true) or *F* (false). Work with a partner. Restate false sentences to make them correct.

_T_ 1. Many plants may become extinct in the future.

___ 2. People are only collecting seeds in England.

___ 3. Seeds are stored in a very warm room in the seed bank.

___ 4. The seeds can be used for medical research.

___ 5. The seed bank is finished collecting seeds.

LISTENING SKILL   Understanding Spoken Numbers

LEARN

It can be difficult to hear and identify numbers when you are listening. Practicing listening for numbers will help you develop this skill. Review the information in the box below, which shows how numbers are spoken.

> 1,000,000,000 = one billion or a billion
>
> 6,700,000 = six million, seven hundred thousand (people, euros)
>
> 1,200 = one thousand, two hundred or twelve hundred
>
> 100 = one hundred or a hundred
>
> 346 = three hundred and forty-six or three hundred forty-six
>
> 25% = twenty-five percent
>
> the year 1995 = nineteen ninety-five
>
> –20° Fahrenheit = minus twenty degrees Fahrenheit

Make sure you can hear and pronounce the differences between numbers like these. Listen for the difference in stress.

13 / 30 = thirteen, thirty

14 / 40 = fourteen, forty

15 / 50 = fifteen, fifty

APPLY

A. Go online to watch the video and listen again. As you listen, complete the sentences below with the numbers you hear.

10%	2020	60,000 to 100,000
25%	one-fifth	a billion

_____ 1. But, _____*60,000 to 100,000*_____ species of plant could disappear.

_____ 2. They have already saved seeds from over _____ of the world's plant species.

_____ 3. Their goal is to collect seeds from _____ of the world's plants by _____ .

_____ 4. Right now, up to _____ of the world's plants are in trouble.

_____ 5. Over a _____ seeds have been banked worldwide, an environmental savings account where each deposit could mean a cure for disease.

B. Work with a partner. Compare your answers. Then practice saying the sentences with the correct numbers. Which numbers are difficult to say and hear?

Vocabulary Activities

A. Replace the words in parentheses with a target word from the box. Use the correct form of the target word. You may use words more than once.

grade	initially	issue	partner	research	resource

This semester in Biology 101, you will work on a special project with a

_____*partner*_____. You will choose a(n) _____ related to the natural
(1. classmate)   (2. problem)

world and _____ it. _____, you will work together to
(3. study carefully)   (4. in the beginning)

decide on your topic. After you choose your topic, you will take about three

weeks to do the _____. I will give you a list of websites that you
(5. careful study)

can consult; the library is also an excellent _____. At the end,
(6. source of information)

you will do a presentation with your _____. This project will count
(7. classmate)

for 50 percent of your final _____.
(8. mark)

B. For the target words below, match the dictionary definitions on the left with the example sentences on the right.

grade (noun)

Definitions

_c_ 1. a letter or number that is given for school work or on an exam

___ 2. one of the levels in a school

___ 3. the quality of a product or level of someone's ability

Example Sentences

a. My brother is excited to start first grade tomorrow.

b. The wood used in the building is of the highest grade.

c. She studied a lot and got good grades last semester.

issue (noun, verb)

Definitions

___ 1. a problem or important topic for discussion

___ 2. one in a series of things that are published or produced

___ 3. to make something known or give out something to the public

Example Sentences

a. Do you have the latest issue of this magazine?

b. The government issued a report on conservation work in the country.

c. Pollution is an issue in many cities.

C. Look at the projects and resources. Which resources are helpful for each project? Can you add any resources? Compare your answers with a partner.

Projects	Resources
1. how to start a garden	a. the Internet
2. a science report for school	b. the library
3. how to cook an unusual dish	c. a newspaper
4. how to learn or start a new hobby or sports activity	d. a TV program
	e. a textbook

The word *initial* means "happening at the beginning." *Initially* is an adverb that means "at the beginning," or at first.

*The **initial** stages of the research project went well. (adj)*

*I liked the job **initially**, but then it got boring. (adv)*

CORPUS

D. Work with a partner. Discuss answers to the questions. Then change partners and discuss again.

1. What is a form or a document that you need to initial?
2. What is something that you liked initially, but then didn't like?
3. What is something that you didn't like initially, but later liked?

The noun *resource* means something that a person, country, or organization, has or can use, especially to increase their wealth.

*My country has a lot of natural **resources**, such as oil and minerals.*

Resourceful is an adjective that means "good at finding ways of doing things."

*She is very **resourceful** in the kitchen. She can make a delicious meal with only a few ingredients.*

CORPUS

E. Work with a partner. Give an example for each use of *resource / resourceful*.

1. what resources you use to do research *The Internet is my main research resource.*

2. a natural resource in your country _____

3. how to be resourceful with money _____

About the Topic

Bees are very important to agriculture. They pollinate plants such as fruits, vegetables, and nuts. This makes it easier and cheaper for farmers to grow crops. However, bee populations are becoming smaller, and scientists don't know exactly why.

Before You Listen

Read these questions. Discuss your answers in a small group.

1. What do you know about bees and their habits?

2. Can you name two ways bees are important in nature?

3. Why might bee conservation be necessary?

Listen

Read the Listen for Main Ideas activity below. Go online to listen to two students who are preparing a presentation on bees for their biology class. They are discussing what information to include in the presentation.

Listen for Main Ideas

Listen to the conversation and answer the questions. Then compare your answers with a partner.

1. What is the specific topic of the students' presentation?

2. What important, positive effect of bees do they want to talk about?

3. Are they going to include a lot of statistics?

4. Are they going to include any photos?

SPEAKING SKILL   Considering Audience for a Presentation

LEARN

Think about your audience when you prepare a presentation. This will help you to present the information in a way that is clear and interesting. Here are some points to help you prepare for a specific audience.

Consider:

1. How much information to include: for example, how long is the presentation?

2. How much knowledge of the topic they have: for example, if you and your classmates are all from the same country, you don't have to explain a lot in a presentation about your country. If your classmates are from different countries, you need to explain more.

3. How much technical information or special language to include: for example, if you're talking about biology, do you need to explain any words the audience might not know?

4. How to organize and present the information to make it clear: for example, is it helpful to include charts, diagrams, or pictures?

5. How formal / informal you should be: for example, are jokes appropriate or not?

APPLY

A. Go online and listen to four parts of the conversation again. Discuss which points from the box on page 32 each one refers to.

B. Work with a partner. Discuss what you would consider for each of these presentation topics. Give reasons for your answers.

1. your favorite vacation location *I would include background information about the location. For example, what activities you can do there, what food is good, and so on. I would explain why I like the place. There would not be specialized language. It would be informal.*

2. a scientific report about plants

3. your perfect job

4. suggestions for how to grow plants

C. Work in small groups. Choose one of the topics from part B and give a three-minute presentation about it. As you listen to your classmates, think about how each person considered the audience in preparing their presentation.

PRONUNCIATION SKILL   Reduced Question Forms

LEARN

You can reduce a question that uses a question word + "do you."

A. Go online to listen to the reduced questions and the example sentences in the chart.

Question word +	do you =	Reduction	Examples
What +	do you / are you =	Whaddaya	**Whaddaya** What do you study? **Whaddaya** What are you planning to research?
Who +	do you =	Whodaya	**Whodaya** Who do you like to study with?
Where +	do you =	Wheredaya	**Wheredaya** Where do you want to go?
When +	do you =	Whendaya	**Whendaya** When do you go home?
Why +	do you =	Whydaya	**Whydaya** Why do you always choose that topic?
How +	do you =	Howdaya	**Howdaya** How do you like the class?

You can also reduce a question that uses a question word + "did you."

🔊 **B.** Go online to listen to the reduced questions and the example sentences in the chart.

Question word +	did you =	Reduction	Examples
What +	did you =	Whadija Whaja	**Whadija** What did you think of the expert's speech?
Who +	did you =	Whodija	**Whodija** Who did you meet yesterday?
Where +	did you =	Wheredija	**Wheredija** Where did you find that resource?
When +	did you =	Whendija	**Whendija** When did you learn so much about gardening?
Why +	did you =	Whydija	**Whydija** Why did you get a low grade in that class?
How +	did you =	Howdija	**Howdija** How did you like the video?

Be careful not to confuse these two reductions. If you hear only the "d" sound, it is the reduction "Whaddaya." If you hear the "j" sound, it is the reduction "Whadija" or "Whaja."

APPLY

🔊 **A.** Go online to listen to the sentences. Circle the reduction that you hear.

1. (Whaddaya)   Whodaya   Whendaya
2. Whodaya   Howdaya   Whaddaya
3. Whydaya   Wheredaya   Whendaya
4. Howdaya   Whendaya   Whaddaya
5. Whaddaya   Whydaya   Whodaya
6. Wheredaya   Whodaya   Howdaya

🔊 **B.** Go online to listen to the sentences. Write the reduction that you hear.

1. _____Howdija_____ work and go to school at the same time?

2. _____ start taking biology classes?

3. _____ think of the presentation?

4. _____ study with after class?

5. _____ choose him as your partner?

6. _____ move here from?

C. With a partner, talk about different ways you can protect the environment. Use reduced question forms with "do you" to ask your partner what he / she is doing.

> A: *Whaddaya want to do for Earth Day this year?*
>
> B: *There's a celebration at the library where they are planting a tree.*
>
> A: *Whodaya think will be interested in starting a garden at school?*
>
> B: *I think many students from our class are interested.*

D. With a partner, talk about trips you have taken to national parks or other outdoor places. Use reduced question forms with "did you" to ask your partner questions about these trips.

> A: *My parents and I went to the Grand Canyon.*
>
> B: *Whendija go?*
>
> A: *We went two years ago.*
>
> B: *Whadija learn about how the Grand Canyon was formed?*

End of Unit Task

In this unit, you learned about seed and bee conservation. You practiced listening for numbers, and you learned about considering audience when preparing a presentation. Apply these skills by listening to some presentations.

A. Go online to listen to extracts from three different presentations about butterfly conservation. Which presentation is for each audience below? Discuss what you think each person considered in preparing the presentation.

1. a group of scientists who all study butterflies *Presentation 3: Her audience has a lot of knowledge about the subject, so she doesn't have to explain specialized language. The presentation is probably quite formal.*

2. a group of school children at a nature center

3. a group of adults who are not scientists

B. Listen again. Write down the numbers that you hear in each presentation.

Presentation 1

- There are about ____24,000____ different species of butterflies in the world.
- Butterfly size can range from less than _____ in size to almost _____ inches.
- One type of butterfly can fly _____ miles per hour.

Presentation 2

- There are _____ teams of volunteers in _____ different regions of the country.

- The average life span of a butterfly is only _____ days.

- Butterflies can't fly if their body temperature is less than _____ degrees Fahrenheit.

Presentation 3

- There were a lot of Karner blue butterflies a hundred years ago, but the population went down _____ in the past century.

- This butterfly lived only in an area between _____ and _____ degrees north latitude.

- We find the Karner blue butterfly in _____ different areas of the United States.

C. Work with a partner to prepare a short presentation on butterflies. Choose an audience for your presentation: classmates in a biology class, classmates in a general class, or grade school children. Remember to think about the points from page 32 for considering the audience.

D. Work in small groups. Give your presentation. Take notes on your classmates' presentations. Pay attention to how they considered the audience.

E. Using your notes, discuss the presentations. How did your classmates consider or not consider the audience when giving their presentations?

Self-Assessment		
Yes	**No**	
☐	☐	I can identify relevant points for various audiences.
☐	☐	I successfully considered the audience when preparing a presentation.
☐	☐	I understand and can identify spoken numbers.
☐	☐	I can pronounce reduced question forms.
☐	☐	I can correctly use the target vocabulary words from the unit.

Discussion Questions

With a partner or in a small group, discuss the following questions.

1. What are some conservation projects in your city or country?

2. What are some natural resources that need to be helped by conservation?

3. What is a topic that you would like to do research on?

UNIT 4

Connected

In this unit, you will
> learn about research into social networks.
> increase your understanding of the target academic words for this unit.

LISTENING AND SPEAKING SKILLS
> Selective Note-Taking
> Opinion Surveys
> **PRONUNCIATION** Tag Questions and Intonation

Self-Assessment
Think about how well you know each target word, and check (✓) the appropriate column. I have…

TARGET WORDS	never seen this word before.	heard or seen the word but am not sure what it means.	heard or seen the word and understand what it means.	used the word confidently in *either* speaking or writing.
AWL				
🔑 achieve				
🔑 couple				
🔑 data				
🔑 document				
🔑 income				
🔑 link				
🔑 objective				
🔑 status				

 Oxford 3000™ keywords

Vocabulary Activities

A. Read the sentences. Cross out the word in parentheses with a different meaning from the other two choices. Use a dictionary to help you understand new words. Compare your answers with a partner.

1. Jun completed his degree. He's very proud of his (*success / achievement / time*).

2. Kaylee and Lars are my next-door neighbors. They are a very nice (*couple / pair / group*).

3. The team's (*practice / goal / objective*) is to win every game this season.

4. The researchers are collecting (*data / information / textbooks*) on health.

5. The goal was to raise $2,000 and we have (*met / lost / achieved*) that goal.

6. A scientific report needs to be (*unclear / fair / objective*).

The verb *achieve* means to reach a particular goal or status.

> You have **achieved** great success in your career.

It also means to complete or accomplish something.

> We have **achieved** a lot in a short time.

The noun is *achievement*.

> Winning the award for best director was her greatest **achievement**.

CORPUS

B. Use one of the collocations with *achieve* or *achievement* below to complete each sentence. Use the correct form of the verb.

academic	a dream	remarkable	success

1. Every parent wants their child to _achieve success_ in school.

2. Climbing Mount Everest at 75 years old is truly a _____.

3. This school has very high _____. The children's test scores are very good.

4. When they bought their own house, my parents _____ that they had for many years.

A couple can mean two people who are in a relationship.

> Lucy and Phillip are getting married! They are such a nice **couple**!

A couple of usually refers to two, or a small number of, things.

> I forgot **a couple of** things.

CORPUS

C. Work in pairs. Ask and answer the questions. In your answer, use the phrase
a couple of and one of the words in the box.

blocks	dollars	minutes	months

1. A: Do you live far from your school?

   B: No, my house is only ___*a couple of blocks*___ away.

2. A: How long have you been living here?

   B: Not long. Just _____ .

3. A: I don't have enough money for a coffee.

   B: Do you want me to lend you _____?

4. A: Are you ready to go?

   B: Yes. I'll be there in _____ .

The word *data* means facts or information, and is usually used in research.
It is a plural noun, but is often used in the singular.

> *The researchers interviewed many people and collected a lot of **data**.*

> *The **data** is / are very interesting.*

 CORPUS

D. Work with a partner. Discuss the best way to get data on each of the following.
Use the ideas in the box.

medical records	observation	school records	surveys

1. how much money students spend each week *To get data on how much money students spend, you could use surveys.*

2. why people go to the doctor's office

3. students' performance on examinations

4. how teenagers spend their free time

The adjective *objective* means "not influenced by personal feelings or opinions."
If you are objective, you consider only facts when making a decision.

> *Please try to give an **objective** report of what happened.*

An *objective* is an aim, goal, or purpose.

> *My **objective** is to graduate next year.*

CORPUS

E. Work with a partner. Talk about the objectives of each item below.

1. recycling paper *The objective of recycling paper is to save trees and have less trash.*

2. dieting

3. playing a game

4. studying English

About the Topic

Social networks are your family, your friends, and your acquaintances. Most people belong to several social networks such as their family and their friends from work or school friends. Sociologists have discovered that these networks have an important influence on our feelings and behavior. Even people we do not know can affect us more than we realize.

Before You Listen

Read these questions. Discuss your answers in a small group.

1. Do you think feelings are contagious? In other words, do your friends' or family's moods and emotions affect you?

2. Do you think your friends can change your behavior, for example, how much you exercise or what you eat?

3. Does your behavior affect your friends and family? If so, how?

Listen

Read the Listen for Main Ideas activity below. Go online to listen to a sociology professor give an informal lecture about social networks.

Listen for Main Ideas

Circle the best answer to complete each sentence.

1. The researchers found that feelings and behavior ____.
    a. cannot be passed between people
    b. can only be passed between people you know well
    c. can be passed between people you don't know well

2. Our emotions are affected more by people who ____.
    a. are nearby
    b. live far away
    c. are both nearby and far away

3. Information for this study came from ____.
    a. a long-term study about people's health
    b. people visiting doctors' offices
    c. people's social networks on the Internet

4. According to the scientists who did the study, we should all try to be happy and healthy because ____.
    a. we will live longer
    b. we will not gain weight
    c. we affect many other people

LEARN

In a lecture, you don't have to write down every piece of information that you hear. Take notes selectively. You may only need to write down the key points—enough to help you study the material later. Key points might include:

- the main point that the speaker is making.
- important names (of authors, studies, researchers).
- important numbers, dates, and places.
- scientific terms (and definitions).

If you don't know how to spell a key word, ask for the spelling or guess and check it later.

APPLY

A. Listen again to part one of the lecture. Then look at the notes below. Notice that the writer only writes the key points that are made.

Part	Notes
1.	*Feelings & behavior can be passed between people in your social networks.*

B. Listen again to part two of the lecture. Then look at the notes. What words are spelled out in full? What words are abbreviated? Why?

Part	Notes
2.	*Christakis & Fowler: researchers: Found that SN's have an imp. effect.*

C. Listen again to parts three to six of the lecture. Stop after each section. Use the questions to help you complete the chart with the key information in each part.

Part	Notes
3.	Who affects our emotions most?
4.	Who can affect our behavior?
5.	How did they gather the data?
6.	What should students do with the data?

Vocabulary Activities

A. Use the following target words to complete the paragraphs below. You will use some words more than once.

achieve	income	objective	status
data	link	objectivity	

Does money make you happy? Scientists decided to research this question.

Their ___*objective*___ was to find a _____ between happiness and
　　　　　(1)　　　　　　　　　　　　(2)

money. They interviewed hundreds of people and collected a lot of

_____. They asked people how happy they were and how much
　(3)

_____ they had. They also asked about the social _____ of
　(4)　　　　　　　　　　　　　　　　　　　　　　　　　　　(5)

each person in the survey: in other words, what their position was in relation

to their friends and family.

Did the scientists _____ their aim? It's difficult to measure "happiness"
　　　　　　　　　　(6)

in a(n) _____ way. So one of the problems was _____. In the
　　　　(7)　　　　　　　　　　　　　　　　　　　　　　(8)

end, the researchers found no clear _____ between happiness and
　　　　　　　　　　　　　　　　　　(9)

_____. In other words, money does not necessarily make people
　(10)

happier.

B. Some of the target words have multiple meanings. For the target words below, match the dictionary definitions on the left with the example sentences on the right. Check your answers with a partner.

document (noun, verb)

Definitions

_c_ 1. an official piece of writing that gives information, proof, or evidence of something

____ 2. a computer file that contains text

____ 3. to record the details of something

Example Sentences

a. The document is too large to send by email.

b. It's important to document all the steps of the project.

c. Please sign this document.

link (noun)

Definitions	Example Sentences
___ 1. a connection between two people or things	a. You can visit other websites by clicking on the link provided.
___ 2. a means of moving or communicating between two places	b. Is there a link between your age and your social status?
___ 3. allows you to connect to a website or document	c. The city opened a new bus link to the airport.

C. Choose two items below and explain how they can be linked.

age	health	job	social status
education	income	physical exercise	

Education is linked to income because if you have more education, you can usually earn more money.

Status can mean your social position in relation to other people.

*Teachers don't have a high **status** in my country.*

Your marital *status* describes whether you are single or married.

*Please indicate your name, age, and marital **status**.*

CORPUS

D. Work with a partner. Discuss the effect of each of the following on (a) your status and (b) your income.

1. getting a job promotion *Getting a job promotion gives you higher status and more income.*
2. buying a new car
3. moving to a smaller apartment or house
4. graduating from a university

E. Describe each of the items below. Use the words *document* and *data* in your descriptions.

1. a passport *A passport is a document that you need for traveling. It includes data about your identity and the countries you have visited.*
2. a birth certificate
3. a degree or a diploma

About the Topic

In the social sciences, a common way to collect data is through the use of questionnaires and surveys. Researchers and students prepare questions and ask as many people as possible. Then they collect and analyze the results.

Before You Watch

Read these questions. Discuss your answers in a small group.

1. Do you think positive or negative emotions spread more easily?

2. Do you think there is a connection between money and happiness?

3. Which is more important to happiness: how much money you have or how many friends you have?

Watch

Read the Listen for Main Ideas activity below. Go online to watch a student interview another student for a sociology class project.

Listen for Main Ideas

Listen to the interview and circle the answers on the survey below. Add comments where necessary to explain your answers.

SOCIAL NETWORKS SURVEY	
To the interviewer: Circle the answers. Add comments to explain.	
1. Can feelings and emotions be contagious?	yes / no / not sure Comment:
2. If yes, which kinds of feelings are more contagious?	positive / negative / not sure Comment:
3. Which is more important to happiness: level of income or number of friends?	level of income / number of friends Comment:
4. Do your friends affect your health habits?	yes / no / not sure Comment:

SPEAKING SKILL Opinion Surveys

LEARN

When you are conducting interviews or surveys, introduce yourself and ask for permission first. Explain the purpose of the questions, and state how long you expect the survey to take.

Here are some useful phrases:

Introducing the survey	Answering questions
Excuse me. I'm doing a survey / some research on ____.	Definitely! Absolutely! Of course!
	I think (that) … / I don't think (that) …
It's for my ____ class.	I'd say that …
The survey / questionnaire is about ____.	I can't say that …
May I ask you some questions?	Hmm, I'm not sure.
Would you mind answering some questions?	I'd rather not answer that question.

APPLY

A. Watch and listen to how the student introduces herself and her survey. Which of the expressions above does she use? Try to write exactly what she says.

Hi, my name is _____ .

It's about _____ .

May I ask you _____ ?

B. Watch and listen to the video again. Write the phrases that the second student uses to introduce her opinion.

Question 1: _____*Oh, definitely!*_____

Question 2: _____

Question 3: _____

Question 4: _____

C. Choose one of the questions from the survey in the listening text and interview three or more classmates. Each time you begin an interview, introduce yourself and explain the purpose of the survey. Use the expressions in the box above.

LEARN

A tag question is a short question at the end of a statement. It can ask the listener to confirm what the speaker is saying. Or, it can ask for the listener's agreement. Intonation, or the rise and fall of your voice when you speak, can change for tag questions depending on the speaker's message.

A. When the speaker is making small talk and wants the listener to agree, the intonation of the tag question falls. Listen to the sentences below.

The objective of the research was interesting, wasn't it?

They are going to help each other get healthier, aren't they?

B. When the speaker is not sure about the statement and wants confirmation from the listener, the intonation of the tag question rises. Go online to listen to these sentences.

Sharing my good news helps others, doesn't it?

My behavior won't affect my friends' behavior, will it?

APPLY

A. Draw the correct intonation arrow above the tag question. Then decide if the speaker is asking for confirmation or agreement by writing "confirmation" or "agreement" after the sentence. Check your answers by listening to the sentences.

1. Your friend's bad mood can affect you, can't it? *agreement*

2. The friends are going to work together, aren't they?

3. The researchers documented their data, didn't they?

4. Social status will affect your health, won't it?

5. Positive thinking among groups of friends is linked to happiness, isn't it?

6. The couple achieved their goal together, didn't they?

B. Say the sentences from activity A with falling intonation on the statements and the correct intonation on the tag questions.

C. Find a partner. Think of three things about that partner that you think you know (where he / she is from, if he / she has a job, etc.), and three things that you would like to know. Use falling intonation on the tag questions for the things you think you know. Use rising intonation on the tag questions for the things you're not sure about. Use the tag questions from the box.

A: You're from California, aren't you?
B: Yes, I am!

A: But you don't work full-time, do you?
B: No, I don't. I have a part-time job.

are / aren't you?	does / doesn't it?	was / wasn't it?	will / won't it?
did / didn't it?	is / isn't it?	were / weren't you?	do / don't you?

End of Unit Task

In this unit, you learned about how people are affected by their social networks. You practiced selective note-taking when listening, and you practiced surveying classmates' opinions. Review these skills by preparing a survey and conducting it outside the classroom.

A. Work with a partner. Choose one of these topics or create your own survey.

friends and social behavior	diet and exercise	use of social media

B. Write a short survey (four questions) to gauge people's opinions on the topic you chose. Questions should begin with *Do you think that* ... ? Use the blank survey form below to write in questions and answers.

SURVEY	
To the interviewer: Circle the answers. Add comments if provided.	
1.	yes / no / not sure Comment:
2.	yes / no / not sure Comment:
3.	yes / no / not sure Comment:
4.	yes / no / not sure Comment:

C. Practice your survey with your classmates. Make changes to your questions if necessary. Use the expressions in the box below.

Introducing the survey	Answering questions
Excuse me. I'm doing a survey / some research on ____.	Definitely! Absolutely! Of course!
It's for my ____ class.	I think (that) … / I don't think (that) …
The survey / questionnaire is about ____.	I'd say that …
May I ask you some questions?	I can't say that …
Would you mind answering some questions?	Hmm, I'm not sure.
	I'd rather not answer that question.

D. Conduct your survey outside the classroom. Remember to practice selective note-taking when you record the answers.

E. Share the results of your survey in a small group.

		Self-Assessment
Yes	**No**	
☐	☐	My partner and I successfully prepared a survey.
☐	☐	I successfully used the expressions for conducting a survey.
☐	☐	I was able to understand and take selective notes on answers to the questions.
☐	☐	I can use tag questions and correct intonation.
☐	☐	I can correctly use the target vocabulary words from the unit.

Discussion Questions

With a partner or in a small group, discuss the following questions.

1. Do you think surveys are useful ways to find out what people think? Why or why not?

2. What people and groups of people are in your social network?

3. Do you use social media to communicate with people in your social network?

UNIT 5

Universal Access

In this unit, you will

> learn about what makes a good university campus.
> increase your understanding of the target academic words for this unit.

LISTENING AND SPEAKING SKILLS

> Directions for Assignments
> Back Channeling
> **PRONUNCIATION** Reduced and Dropped Vowels

Self-Assessment

Think about how well you know each target word, and check (✓) the appropriate column. I have…

TARGET WORDS	never seen this word before.	heard or seen the word but am not sure what it means.	heard or seen the word and understand what it means.	used the word confidently in *either* speaking or writing.
AWL				
🔑 access				
🔑 aid				
🔑 code				
🔑 expand				
🔑 fee				
🔑 file				
🔑 site				
🔑 task				

🔑 Oxford 3000™ keywords

Vocabulary Activities

A. In each of the sentences below, cross out the word in parentheses with a different meaning from the other two choices.

1. The School of Business is (*expanding / ~~falling~~ / growing*) and there is not enough space for all of the students. Because of this, the school is moving to a larger (*location / site / office*) at the end of next year.

2. On my first day in the office, my most important (*job / time / task*) was to organize the (*desks / files / papers*) to make it easier for the staff to find information.

B. Match the definitions on the left with the example sentences on the right.

> file (noun, verb)

Definitions

_c_ 1. a folded piece of thick paper for keeping loose papers together

___ 2. a collection of data stored in a computer under one name

___ 3. to put documents in a place so that you can find them easily

Example Sentences

a. Click on the file labeled "Homework" to open it.

b. Please file this letter under "Job Applications."

c. There were so many files on the desk that there was no space to work.

> site (noun)

Definitions

___ 1. a piece of land that is or will be used for a building

___ 2. a place where something happened in the past

___ 3. a place online where you can find information

Example Sentences

a. This link will take you to another Internet site for more information.

b. There is a plan to develop the site next to the hospital.

c. The tourists visited the site of a Civil War battle.

C. Write the target word from the box that works best with the phrases below.

> expansion   file   site   task

1. to have, keep, review, update, check a _____*file*_____

2. great, dramatic, international, economic _____

3. a web, construction, possible, historical _____

4. an easy, difficult, challenging, dangerous _____

To *expand* is to become greater in size, number, or importance.

*Metals **expand** when they are heated.*

*We hope to **expand** our business next year.*

The noun is *expansion*, an act of making something increase.

*The government has announced an **expansion** of its economic program.*

CORPUS

D. **Work with a partner. Say which of the following you think are expanding in your city or country and why.**

universities *Universities are expanding because people need higher education.*

cities

the population

shopping centers

travel opportunities

access to the Internet

public transportation

E. **Look at the list of tasks on the left. Match each task with an appropriate adjective on the right. Then make sentences using the word *task*. Be prepared to explain your answers.**

Learning a language can be a difficult task.

Learning a language	challenging
Doing laundry	difficult
Making a sandwich	important
Reading a website in English	enjoyable
Giving someone bad news	time-consuming
Taking the bus	unpleasant
Talking to an English speaker	routine
Planning a vacation	simple

F. **Discuss the following questions with a partner.**

1. What kind of files do you have on your computer?
2. What information do you keep in paper files? Why?
3. Why is it important to back up your files on the computer?
4. What are some ways to send a large electronic file (for example, an audio or video file) to someone else?
5. What are some important historical sites that you know?
6. What construction sites are in your area? What is being built there?
7. What websites do you use most often?

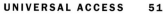

About the Topic

Careful design of a university campus helps to give it a pleasant atmosphere. Designers plan how students will move between buildings, and how to manage traffic. They also plan good public spaces to help make the campus an attractive place to work and study.

Before You Listen

Read these questions. Discuss your answers in a small group.

1. Describe the campus or school where you study. What do you like about it? What would you like to change about it?

2. What makes a university campus attractive for students and teachers?

3. Think of a public place you know that is a popular place for people to meet. Why do you think people go there?

Listen

Read the Listen for Main Ideas activity below. Go online to listen to a lecture about what makes a good university campus.

Listen for Main Ideas

Using your notes, choose the correct answer according to the information in the lecture. Compare your answers with a partner. Listen again if necessary.

1. A university campus is like a small town because ____.
   a. they have the same kinds of problems
   b. they have the same number of people
   c. they both have a lot of parks

2. According to the lecturer, a university campus should not have too many ____.
   a. buses
   b. cars
   c. bicycles

3. Good public spaces are important on a university campus because ____.
   a. students need places to eat
   b. students and teachers need places to meet
   c. lecture halls are too small

4. The students have to prepare a report about ____.
   a. the lecture
   b. their town
   c. their campus

LEARN

In class, lecturers and professors often give directions for assignments orally. When this happens, listen closely and write down what you have to do. Listen for the following information:

1. What exactly do you have to do?
2. What do you have to produce and how much?
3. In what format should you give your work to the professor?
4. When is the assignment due?
5. What other directions does the professor give?

APPLY

A. Here are some possible answers to the five questions above. Write the number of the question (1–5) next to each answer.

1. It's due on Monday.   Question: ___4___
2. We have to upload our work to the class site.   Question: _____
3. We have to write a summary of a chapter in the textbook. Question: _____
4. We have to write about 300 words.   Question: _____
5. Before we hand it in, we have to check the spelling.   Question: _____

B. Go online to listen to the last part of the lecture again. Note the answers to the five questions below.

1. What exactly do you have to do? *Look at this campus. Consider (a) traffic and transportation and (b) public spaces.*

2. What do you have to produce and how much? _____

3. In what format should you give your work to the professor? _____
_____

4. When is the assignment due? _____

5. What other directions does the professor give? _____

C. Compare your answers with a partner. Did you write down the same information?

Vocabulary Activities

A *code* is a system of letters, numbers, or symbols used to pass messages and information in secret.

> *The twins communicated using a* **code** *that only they could understand.*

A *code* is also a set of rules or laws for behavior.

> *The building* **code** *does not allow high buildings in this area.*

CORPUS

A. Complete each sentence with one of the collocations of *code* below.

area	building	postal	secret	security

1. You have to dial the _security code_ to enter the building.

2. The police could not understand the message because it was written in a special _____ .

3. According to the _____ , this store needs to have two exits.

4. Write the _____ clearly on the package so that it reaches the right address.

5. My telephone number is 555-8701. The _____ for my city is 213.

B. The words in bold have more than one meaning, depending on context. Read the sentences and circle the meaning that best fits the context.

1. You have to take this elevator to **access** the upper floors.

   a. to reach a place   b. to be able to use something

2. I can't seem to **access** my files on this computer.

   a. to reach a place   b. to be able to use something

3. I'm applying for financial **aid** to pay my tuition.

   a. help   b. money, food, etc., that is given to people to help them

4. I managed to find my way with the **aid** of a map.

   a. help   b. money, food, etc., that is given to people to help them

5. You can ask a lawyer for advice, but he / she will charge you a **fee**.

   a. money you pay for professional services   b. the cost of an exam, membership, etc.

6. There is a registration **fee** of $50 to join the sports club.

   a. money you pay for professional services   b. the cost of an exam, membership, etc.

Word Form Chart		
Noun	**Verb**	**Adjective**
access accessibility	access	accessible inaccessible

C. Using the target words in the Word Form Chart, complete these sentences. Be sure to use the correct form of each word.

1. Many people do not have _____access_____ to clean water.

2. Some places in the Arctic are only _____ in summer.

3. The new wheelchair ramp will improve _____ for disabled people.

4. After the earthquake, the mountain village was _____ for days.

D. Match the items on the left with what they provide access to on the right. Make sentences with these phrases using the word *access*. *She left her key to give her sister access to her house.*

_c_ 1. A key   a. the Internet

___ 2. An elevator   b. the upper floors of a building

___ 3. A bank card   c. a house or apartment

___ 4. A computer   d. your bank account

E. Select a word in the second column and a phrase from the last column to create an accurate sentence. *A bar code identifies a product in a computer.*

_d_ 1. A bar   aid / (code)   a. helps students to pay for their education.

___ 2. Financial   aid / code   b. helps a person before the EMTs arrive.

___ 3. A postal   aid / code   c. helps people find your address.

___ 4. First   aid / code   d. identifies a product in a computer.

F. Work with a partner. Answer the questions. Use the word *aid* in your answer.

1. How can you see if you don't have good eyesight? *If you don't have good eyesight, you can see with the aid of glasses.*

2. How can you find your way in a new place?

3. How can you understand a word in a foreign language?

G. Work with a partner. Discuss who or what might charge each type of fee, and in what situation. Which of these fees have you paid?

> *The government charges auto registration fees when you buy a car.*

auto registration fees   baggage fees

tuition fees   late fees

membership fees   legal fees

About the Topic

On campus, students usually walk, ride a bike, or take a shuttle bus from one class to another. People in wheelchairs also need to get around. By law, public buildings and transportation in the U.S. must be accessible to wheelchairs.

Before You Listen

Read these questions. Discuss your answers in a small group.

1. How do you travel to school or work? Why do you use this type of transportation?

2. How easy is it for people in wheelchairs to access different parts of your school or workplace?

Listen

Read the Listen for Main Ideas activity below. Go online to listen to a discussion among a group of students. They are preparing a group report for their urban studies class.

Listen for Main Ideas

Work with a partner to number the topics below in the order they are discussed.

____ Asking Patrick's opinion   ____ Accessibility for wheelchairs

____ Parking on campus   ____ Taking the bus

SPEAKING SKILL   Back Channeling

LEARN

In conversations and group discussions, people show that they understand and are interested in a conversation by using expressions such as *right, I know,* or *uh-huh.* This is called back channeling, and it helps to keep a conversation going. After back channeling, people often say more to add to a conversation.

Expressions for back channeling	Examples
Showing agreement: Uh-huh. / Yeah. / Right. / I know.	A: The fees for the parking permit are so high. B: **Yeah. I know.**
Showing agreement (negative): No.	A: I don't really know much about it. B: **No.** Me neither.
Showing interest: Hmm. / Really? / I see.	A: My friend Patrick ... has a hard time getting around. B: **Really?**

APPLY

A. Go online to listen to the audio again. Count the expressions for back channeling that you hear. Which one is used the most in this conversation?

B. Read the following section of the conversation. The back channeling expressions have been taken out. Try to guess the words that are missing. Then listen and check your answers.

S1: Is it easy for people in wheelchairs to access the classrooms and buildings? What do you think?

S2: I think it's pretty good.

S3: (1.) _Yeah_. It looks like people can get around campus with the aid of wheelchair ramps and elevators. But I don't really know much about it.

S2: (2.) ___. Me neither.

S4: Well, actually, my friend Patrick uses a wheelchair, and I think he has a hard time getting around.

S1: (3.) ___? Why is that?

S4: Well, the classrooms have to be accessible to wheelchairs. That's the law. It's in the building code. But some of the buildings aren't easy to access.

S1: (4.) ___. That's interesting. Which ones?

S4: Sometimes he has to go to Washington Hall. It's an old building. There's only one elevator, and it's at the back of the building, so it takes a long time to get to the classrooms.

S2: Oh, (5.) ___. That's not good.

S4: (6.) ___. Maybe I could ask him about his experience.

S1: That would be great. It would be really nice to get his opinion on this.

S3: (7.) ___. Good idea!

S4: OK. I'll text him right now.

C. Read or listen to the conversation again. What do the speakers add to the conversation after they back channel?

D. Insert appropriate back channeling expressions into the conversation below, and add a short response. Practice the conversation with a partner. Then switch roles.

A: I usually drive to work.

B: (1.) _Really? / Yeah. So do I. / Me too._

A: It's just so convenient.

B: (2.) _____

A: But the traffic is terrible.

B: (3.) _____

A: Sometimes it takes me more than an hour to get to work.

B: (4.) _____

A: But there's no public transportation. So I don't have a choice.

B: (5.) _____

LEARN

Vowel sounds can be stressed or unstressed. The vowel sound in the unstressed syllables of a word may be reduced or dropped when spoken.

A. In Unit 1, you learned about stressed and unstressed syllables. The stressed syllable in a word is pronounced longer, stronger, and higher than the other syllables in the word. Go online to listen to the examples. Notice the stressed syllables in pink.

ac•cess	se•**mes**•ter
ex•**pand**	u•ni•**ver**•si•ty

The unstressed syllables in a word can sometimes be reduced to the /ə/ sound.

B. Go online to listen to the examples. Notice that the vowel sound is reduced to the /ə/ sound.

at•mŏs•phere	dĕ•**sign**
cŏn•**trol**	ŏ•pi•nion

The vowel sound of an unstressed syllable can also be dropped in some words. This means the word loses a syllable.

C. Go online to listen to the words. Notice which words are *usually* said with the dropped syllable, and which words are *sometimes* said with a dropped syllable.

Word	Dropped vowel sound	Sounds like ...	Always or sometimes?
basically	basically	ba•si•cly	Always
camera	camera	cam•ra	Always
chocolate	chocolate	cho•clate	Always
different	different	diff•rent	Always
evening	evening	ev•ning	Always
favorite	favorite	fav•rite	Always
especially	especially	es•pesh•ly	Sometimes
family	family	fam•ly	Sometimes
history	history	his•try	Sometimes

APPLY

A. Go online to listen to the following words. Draw a slash through the unstressed syllables with the /ə/ sound. Work with a partner to check your answers.

1. dis•a•bi•li•ty
2. e•le•va•tor
3. at•trac•tive
4. ac•cess•i•bil•i•ty
5. u•ni•ver•si•ty
6. pro•duce

B. Go online to listen to the following words. Underline the syllable with the dropped vowel sound. Work with a partner to check your answers.

1. com•<u>for</u>•ta•ble
2. res•taur•ant
3. ex•tra•or•di•nar•y
4. sev•er•al
5. gen•er•al•ly
6. ev•er•y
7. a•ver•age
8. in•ter•es•ting

C. Say the words in activities B and C in the Learn section above. Reduce the appropriate vowel to the /ə/ sound, or drop the vowel sound where appropriate.

D. With a partner, write questions about your school's campus to elicit opinions. In every question, use one or two words where the vowel is reduced to the /ə/ sound or dropped. Use the words in the word box in your responses.

A: Do you think the design of the buildings is interesting?
B: I suppose so, but it's more important that the classrooms are comfortable.

atmosphere	design	every	interesting
attractive	different	favorite	opinion
average	especially	generally	

End of Unit Task

In this unit, you have learned how to understand directions for a class assignment, and how to use back channeling to keep a conversation going. Review these skills by taking notes on some assignments, and by participating in a discussion with your classmates.

A. Go online to listen to the homework assignments. For each assignment, take notes on what you have to do. Consider these questions. (You will not use all of the questions for each assignment.)

1. What exactly do you have to do?
2. What do you have to produce and how much?
3. In what format should you give your work to the professor?
4. When is the assignment due?
5. What other directions does the professor give?

B. Compare notes with a partner. Did your notes contain the same information?

C. Discuss the assignments with a partner. Which assignment is the easiest? The most difficult? The most useful? Use back channeling expressions in your conversation.

Expressions for back channeling	Examples
Showing agreement: Uh-huh. / Yeah. / Right. / I know.	A: The fees for the parking permit are so high. B: **Yeah. I know.**
Showing agreement (negative): No.	A: I don't really know much about it. B: **No.** Me neither.
Showing interest: Hmm. / Really? / I see.	A: My friend Patrick … has a hard time getting around. B: **Really?**

D. Work in small groups. Discuss the questions below. During the discussion, try to use some of the back channeling expressions above.

1. How does your school, university, or town make places more accessible for wheelchairs?
2. Is there too much traffic in your city? What would be a good way to change this?
3. Do you use public transportation to get around? Why or why not?

Self-Assessment		
Yes	**No**	
☐	☐	I successfully understood the directions for class assignments.
☐	☐	In partner discussions, I used back channeling to keep the conversation going.
☐	☐	In the group discussion, I used back channeling to keep the conversation going.
☐	☐	I can understand reduced and dropped vowel sounds.
☐	☐	I can correctly use the target vocabulary words from the unit.

Discussion Questions

With a partner or in a small group, discuss the following questions.

1. Imagine no cars are allowed on your school's campus. How would it be different?
2. As populations expand, how will urban design change?
3. Are you good at giving directions for tasks? Explain your answer.

UNIT 6

Food Choices

In this unit, you will

> learn about the history of restaurants.
> increase your understanding of the target academic words for this unit.

LISTENING AND SPEAKING SKILLS

> Using a T-Chart to Take Notes
> Beginning a Presentation
> **PRONUNCIATION** Can and Can't

Self-Assessment

Think about how well you know each target word, and check (✓) the appropriate column. I have…

TARGET WORDS	never seen this word before.	heard or seen the word but am not sure what it means.	heard or seen the word and understand what it means.	used the word confidently in *either* speaking or writing.
AWL				
🔑 conclude				
🔑 focus				
🔑 item				
🔑 lecture				
🔑 normal				
🔑 plus				
🔑 relax				
🔑 topic				

🔑 Oxford 3000™ keywords

Vocabulary Activities

A. Read the restaurant review. Cross out the word in parentheses with a different meaning from the other two. Use a dictionary to help you understand new words. Compare answers with a partner.

There's a new restaurant in town called Alexi's. There are many 1. (*items / prices / things*) on the menu, and all of the food is good. You don't need to dress up because the atmosphere is 2. (*exciting / informal / relaxed*). The restaurant looks expensive, so you might 3. (*agree / believe / conclude*) that the food costs a lot, but it doesn't. The prices are quite 4. (*cheap / normal / typical*).

Word Form Chart			
Noun	**Verb**	**Adjective**	**Adverb**
normality	normalize	normal	normally
relaxation	relax	relaxed	_____
conclusion	conclude	conclusive	conclusively
item	itemize	_____	_____

B. Complete the following sentences using the words from the Word Form Chart. Be sure to use the correct form and tense of each word.

1. The store receipt ___*itemizes*___ everything you buy.

2. I always feel very _____ after my vacation.

3. I need to buy some food. There are a lot of _____ on my shopping list.

4. _____, we eat at home, but we sometimes eat out on Fridays.

5. The doctor's office is open during _____ office hours.

6. After the semester is over, I am going to the beach for a few days of _____ .

7. From the research, scientists reached the _____ that many people do not have healthy eating habits.

C. Match a word on the left with a collocation on the right. Then use the phrases to complete the sentences.

back to	perfectly	relax	item
individual	reach	a conclusion	normal

1. Each _individual item_ was carefully packed so that it wouldn't break.

2. Don't worry. It's _____ to feel tired after a long day at school.

3. We need to do more tests before we can _____ .

4. The teachers were very busy before exams but now things are _____ .

To *conclude* is "to decide or believe something as a result of what you have heard or seen." To *reach a conclusion* has a similar meaning.

> The scientists **concluded** that the medication helped 68 percent of the patients.

> After reading the study, we **reached the conclusion** that the treatment was successful.

To *conclude* also means to bring to an end. *To conclude*, or *in conclusion*, is often used in formal speeches or academic papers.

> **To conclude / In conclusion**, I'd like to offer you some advice.

CORPUS

D. Work with a partner. Say what conclusion you might reach in each of the following cases.

1. There is a line of people outside a popular restaurant.
   You might reach the conclusion that the restaurant is very popular.
2. Your teacher does not come to class.
3. People outside are carrying umbrellas.
4. An ambulance goes by with the lights flashing.

E. Define each item on the left using a phrase on the right. Then discuss the questions below with a partner.

_d_ 1. a chair

____ 2. a diamond ring

____ 3. a story about a lost child

____ 4. a shirt

____ 5. pots, pans, and plates

____ 6. a postage stamp from 1800

a. an item of clothing

b. a collector's item

c. a luxury item

d. an item of furniture

e. a news item

f. household items

1. What items of clothing do you buy regularly?
2. What news item is popular this week?
3. What luxury item would you like to own?

F. Below are some different things that people do in restaurants. Work with a partner. Say which of the following are normal where you live and which are not.

1. order from a menu *It's normal to order from a menu at a restaurant.*
2. drink water with your meal
3. give a tip to the waiter
4. pay before you eat
5. snap your fingers to call a waiter
6. take extra food home with you
7. talk to the people at other tables

About the Topic

Eating at restaurants is a common activity in many places today. But restaurants have not always existed. Before restaurants, the only place to eat outside the home was at an inn: a place for travelers to stop and eat. Later, restaurants gained popularity because, unlike inns, they offered a variety of dishes.

Before You Listen

Read these questions. Discuss your answers in a small group.

1. Describe a restaurant you like. What do you like about it?
2. How is eating at a restaurant different from eating at home?
3. What are some things that all restaurants have in common?

Listen

Read the Listen for Main Ideas activity below. Go online to listen to a podcast about the history of restaurants. The speaker talks about how restaurants began and how a restaurant was different from an inn.

Listen for Main Ideas

Mark each sentence as *T* (true) or *F* (false). Work with a partner. Restate false sentences to make them correct.

_F_ 1. The word "restaurant" originally described a place.

____ 2. Restaurants and inns were very different.

____ 3. At an inn, you could choose what you wanted to eat.

____ 4. At an inn, you paid for your seat at the table not your food.

____ 5. Restaurants existed in China in the thirteenth century.

LEARN

In a T-chart, you organize information into two columns. This kind of chart is useful for comparing and contrasting, for summarizing advantages and disadvantages, or for describing causes and effects.

Look at this example of a T-chart showing the advantages and disadvantages of eating out.

Advantages of eating out	Disadvantages of eating out
Don't have to cook	Can be expensive!
Can try different kinds of food	Some new and unusual foods don't taste good.

A. Look at the T-chart with information from the lecture. Think about what information is missing.

Differences between restaurants and inns	
Restaurants	**Inns**
Had menus	No choice: you ate what they served
You knew what food you were going to get	You took what (1) _____.
(2) _____	Visitors not treated as well as local people
Could eat with friends or family	(3) _____

B. Listen to the lecture again. Complete the T-chart in activity A.

C. Work with a partner. Use your T-charts to summarize the differences between restaurants and inns.

In restaurants they had menus, but at inns, you ate what they were serving.

Vocabulary Activities

A. Complete the paragraph using the words or phrases in the box. Be sure to use the correct form and tense of each target word.

focus on	lecture	lecturer	plus	topic	topical

How would you like to be able to continue your education in your own home?

With a course from University for All, you can do that. You can download

thousands of ___*lectures*___ on a variety of interesting _____.
                  (1. talks)   (2. subjects)

One popular course is called Nutrition for Everyone. This course

_____ healthy eating and nutrition. We also study _____ issues
 (3. examines)   (4. popular)

such as low-fat diets. All of our _____ are experts. _____, all
                                    (5. speakers)   (6. and)

new students will receive a set of course materials absolutely free!

B. For the target vocabulary word below, match the dictionary definitions on the left with the example sentences on the right.

focus

Definitions

_b_ 1. added to (mathematics)

____ 2. to adjust your camera or your eyes to clearly see something

____ 3. to give all your attention to something

Example Sentences

a. Today we're going to focus on healthy eating habits.

b. The main focus of the class is healthy eating.

c. This camera will automatically focus on a person's face.

plus

Definitions

____ 1. added to (mathematics)

____ 2. an advantage

____ 3. in addition

Example Sentences

a. My new school is near my home, which is a big plus.

b. There is no school tomorrow. Plus, it's my birthday!

c. Two plus two equals four.

EVENING LECTURE SERIES

Friday, May 8, 7:00–9:00 p.m., Washington Hall
Prof. Marcus Anderson: Eating Well and Staying Healthy

Friday, May 15, 7:30–9:00 p.m., Lincoln Hall
Prof. Margaret Hall: Fast Food and Nutrition: Can You Have Both?

Friday, May 22, 7:00–8:00 p.m., Pine Lodge
Prof. Jane Wong: Vegetarian Diets for the Twenty-first Century

C. **Work with a partner. Together, answer the questions about the lecture on May 8. Then ask and answer questions about the remaining two events.**

1. Where is the lecture on May 8? *It's at Washington Hall.*
2. Who is the lecturer?
3. What is the topic?
4. When does the lecture start?
5. When does the lecture end?

D. **A *plus* can mean an advantage. The opposite is a *minus*, which is a disadvantage. Discuss the pluses and minuses of the following in small groups.**

1. a big house

   The pluses of a big house are that there is a lot of space and everyone could have a room. A minus is that there would be more rooms to clean.
2. a fast car
3. having brothers and sisters
4. living in the city

E. **Work with a partner. Give examples of these things for the different groups.**

an interesting topic of conversation	a boring topic of conversation
a good lecture topic	a boring lecture topic

1. university students

   For university students, an interesting topic of conversation would be what to do on the weekend.
2. school children
3. business people
4. art students

F. **Work in small groups. Discuss the questions.**

1. What is your favorite topic of conversation?
2. What is not an interesting topic for you?
3. What is something you've focused a lot on in your life?

About the Topic

People's diets often change as their lives change. For example, when students leave home to live and study in a different city or country, their eating habits may change dramatically. They may eat less healthy food and more fast food.

Before You Watch

Read these questions. Discuss your answers in a small group.

1. Have your eating habits changed as you've grown older? Why or why not?

2. How do you think students who live away from home eat differently from the way they do at home?

3. What are some reasons that people snack and eat fast food?

Watch

Read the Listen for Main Ideas activity below. Go online to watch a student give a presentation about eating habits among international students.

Listen for Main Ideas

Watch the presentation. Check (✓) the three changes in eating habits that the student describes.

____ 1. eating a wider variety of kinds of food

____ 2. eating more fast food

____ 3. eating fewer fruits and vegetables

____ 4. having food delivered

____ 5. snacking and eating between meals

PRESENTATION SKILL Beginning a Presentation

LEARN

When you are beginning a presentation, you need to get your audience's attention and make them interested in what you have to say. Here are some suggestions.

1. Before you begin, scan the whole audience. Look at individuals in different parts of the room. Smile. Wait until you have their attention before you start.

2. Use a "hook" to begin your presentation. A hook is a technique to get the audience interested.

Common hooks
Show a picture related to the topic.
Bring in an item related to the topic.
Ask a question.
Tell a story.
Share a surprising fact.
Use a quotation from a famous person.

APPLY

A. Go online and watch the presentation again. What kind of hook did the student use? Did it work? Why or why not?

B. Work with a partner. Read the examples of different hooks that students used to begin their presentations. Discuss what you think the presentations might have been about.

1. Sam showed statistics about the numbers of students studying overseas.

   Maybe the presentation was about studying overseas, or about the problems of international students.

2. Reiko showed a photograph of her grandmother.

3. Xiao asked his classmates what Chinese dishes they were familiar with.

4. Lia told a well-known story from her country about a rich man who lost his money.

5. Donald opened with a quote from Gandhi: "You must be the change you wish to see in the world."

C. Think of a good hook for each of the following presentations. Then compare your ideas in small groups.

1. how to make a favorite dish

2. results of a survey about students' use of free time

3. cheap places to eat in my city

4. a personal story about a frightening experience

5. a person who influenced me

D. Continue working together in your small groups. Using the common hook suggestions in the box above, and your ideas from activity B, take turns giving the beginning of a presentation. Then discuss which hook was most effective in creating interest and why.

LEARN

Can and *can't* may be pronounced in different ways.

In Unit 5, you learned about reducing vowel sounds to the /ə/ sound in unstressed syllables. The vowel sound in *can* is often reduced to this /ə/ sound. This makes *can* short and difficult to hear.

 A. Go online to listen to the sentences.

1. We **can** celebrate her birthday at a restaurant.

2. You **can** try to change your eating habits.

When *can* is at the end of a sentence, the vowel sound usually is not reduced. It is pronounced with the vowel sound /æ/, like the *a* in *mat*. It also is stressed.

B. Listen to the sentence.

Yes, I **can**.

Can't also is pronounced with the vowel sound /æ/. When a consonant sound follows the word *can't*, pause briefly (|), before making the next sound. When *can't* is followed by a vowel sound, the *t* sound changes to *d*.

C. Listen to the sentences. Notice that *can't* is longer than *can* and easier to hear. Also notice that the word *can't* is stressed but is stressed less than the pink focus words in the sentence. When it comes at the end of the sentence, it is stressed like a focus word.

1. Eating in expensive restaurants is something we **can't** | do all the time.

2. I **can't** | eat fast food because it makes me sick.

3. No, I **can't**.

D. Listen to the question twice, once with the reduced vowel and once with the vowel sound /æ/.

Can we conclude from the article that nutrition should be taught in schools?

APPLY

A. Listen to the sentences. Write *can* or *can't* on the blank, depending on what is used in the sentence. Check your answers.

1. He _____*can*_____ order the salad plus a main course.

2. The lecture _____ be in the new auditorium.

3. I _____ buy the food for the party by myself.

4. Rafael _____ cook traditional meals using his mother's recipes.

LISTENING TIPS

1. If you hear a clear /æ/ sound and a pause, you're probably hearing *can't*.

2. If you don't hear much and the connection is smooth, you're probably hearing *can*.

5. I _____ get used to the food in a different country easily.

6. She _____ eat when she's walking from class to class.

In questions, *can* may be pronounced with the reduced vowel or with the vowel sound /æ/.

B. Say the sentences in Learn activities A, B, and C. Reduce the vowel sound in *can* to the /ə/ sound. Pronounce the vowel sound in *can't* like /æ/, the *a* sound in *mat*. Pause briefly (|) after *can't*. Stress the focus word the most.

C. With a partner, ask questions about what kinds of food he / she can make. Use the correct pronunciations of *can* and *can't*. When asking a question, use either the /ə/ sound or the /æ/ sound. Pause briefly (|) after *can't*.

> A: Can you make your own tomato sauce?
>
> B: No, I can't. But I can ask my mother to teach me how.

End of Unit Task

In this unit, you practiced making and using a T-chart to organize your notes. You also practiced ways to start a presentation, including creating a good "hook" to engage the audience. Review these skills by making another T-chart and doing a short presentation.

A. Go online and watch Mike's presentation again. Take notes and organize your notes on a T-chart.

Changes in eating habits for international students	
Before moving	After moving
· ate less fast food	

B. Work with a partner. Compare your T-charts. Did you make a note of the same changes in eating habits?

C. Choose a topic from the list below, or use your own idea. Prepare a presentation (two to three minutes) on the topic. Make notes about what you will say. Make sure you plan a hook to engage your audience. Review the different types of hooks on page 69 or 72.

my eating habits as a child and now

typical food in one country and in another

two places to eat: how they are different

my life in the past and my life now

my life and someone else's life (a family member, friend, celebrity)

1. Before you begin, scan the whole audience. Look at individuals in different parts of the room. Smile. Wait until you have their attention before you start.

2. Use a "hook" to begin your presentation. A hook is a technique to get the audience interested.

Common hooks
Show a picture related to the topic.
Bring in an item related to the topic.
Ask a question.
Tell a story.
Share a surprising fact.
Use a quotation from a famous person.

D. Work in small groups. Take turns giving your presentations.

E. As you listen, take notes on your classmates' presentations. Use a T-chart to organize your notes.

F. Compare and discuss your notes with your group. Do your T-charts include all the important points the presenter made? Were the hooks used in each presentation appropriate? Did they interest the audience?

Self-Assessment		
Yes	**No**	
☐	☐	I successfully used a T-chart to take notes.
☐	☐	I used a hook at the beginning of my presentation.
☐	☐	I used eye contact and waited to get the attention of the audience before starting my presentation.
☐	☐	I understand *can* and *can't* and pronounce them correctly.
☐	☐	I can correctly use the target vocabulary words from the unit.

Discussion Questions

With a partner or in a small group, discuss the following questions.

1. Do you prefer to eat meals at home or in restaurants? Explain your answer.

2. How do you make food choices? Are your choices based on eating healthy, convenience, taste, cost, or other factors?

3. In class, do you prefer lectures or activities and discussion? Why?

UNIT 7

A Good Slogan

In this unit, you will

> learn about the importance of branding, slogans, and logo design.

> increase your understanding of the target academic words for this unit.

LISTENING AND SPEAKING SKILLS

> Listening for Signpost Phrases in a Lecture

> Using Signpost Phrases in a Short Presentation

> **PRONUNCIATION** Sequence Words and Phrases

Self-Assessment

Think about how well you know each target word, and check (✓) the appropriate column. I have...

TARGET WORDS	never seen this word before.	heard or seen the word but am not sure what it means.	heard or seen the word and understand what it means.	used the word confidently in *either* speaking or writing.
AWL				
🔑 acknowledge				
🔑 enormous				
🔑 found				
🔑 goal				
🔑 highlight				
🔑 minor				
🔑 positive				
🔑 purchase				

🔑 Oxford 3000™ keywords

Vocabulary Activities

Word Form Chart			
Noun	**Verb**	**Adjective**	**Adverb**
acknowledgement	acknowledge	_____	_____
enormity	_____	enormous	enormously
founder	found	_____	_____
purchaser	purchase	_____	_____

A. Replace the words in parentheses with a target word from the Word Form Chart. Use the correct form and tense of the target words.

1. The business was (*started*) ___*founded*___ in 1964.

2. The (*person who established the business*) _____ was a man named Theodore Stilton.

3. In 1982, the business was (*bought*) _____ by my grandfather.

4. He was (*very*) _____ successful.

5. However, in 2004, he had to (*admit*) _____ that he was losing money.

6. So he looked for someone to (*buy*) _____ the company.

B. Identify the correct meaning of *acknowledge* in each of the sentences below.

a. to accept that something is real or true
b. to show that you have noticed someone
c. to indicate that you have received a letter, email, etc.

__*a*__ 1. We have to acknowledge that the advertising campaign is not working.

____ 2. I saw Tom at the meeting, but he didn't acknowledge me.

____ 3. I sent my daughter a gift, but she hasn't acknowledged it.

____ 4. The company acknowledged its mistake and changed the design.

C. Write the target word from the box that works best with the phrases below. Then add one phrase to each item.

enormous	goal	positive	purchase

1. __enormous__ influence, responsibility, task

   an enormous house

2. _____ an expensive, an important, an online

   _____

3. _____ reach a, score a, set a, the ultimate

   _____

4. _____ attitude, opinion, results, response

   _____

D. Work with a partner. Say these sentences in another way. Use a form of *acknowledge*.

1. The manager said that he had made a mistake.

   The manager acknowledged that he had made a mistake.

2. We know that many people disagree with us.

   _____

3. After the speech, the president smiled and waved at the crowd.

   _____

4. The researcher admitted that he had not solved the problem.

   _____

E. Work with a partner to match the items on the left with the dates and places where each was founded.

_b_ 1. Google   a. 1976, Cupertino, California

___ 2. McDonald's Corporation   b. 1998, Menlo Park, California

___ 3. Apple Inc.   c. 1945, San Francisco, California

___ 4. The United Nations   d. 1937, Japan

___ 5. Toyota Motor Corporation   e. 1940, San Bernardino, California

F. Work with a partner. Ask and answer the questions below. Then continue the conversation.

1. Who or what had an enormous influence on your life?

    A: My grandmother had an **enormous influence** on my life because I lived with her during my childhood. What about you?

    B: Well, my ...

2. What is an enormous challenge for a student of English?

    _____

3. What musician do you think has had enormous success?

    _____

4. What innovation has had an enormous impact on our lifestyles?

    _____

About the Topic

A brand is the image of a product that makes it stand out. Successful businesses and organizations use slogans, logos, and advertising campaigns to promote their brand. This makes the brand stronger and easier to recognize.

Before You Listen

Read these questions. Discuss your answers in a small group.

1. What is a brand?
2. What brand names do you know?
3. Why do you think a city might want to create a brand for itself?

Listen

Read the Listen for Main Ideas activity below. Go online to listen to a professor describe the process of creating a brand for a city.

Listen for Main Ideas

As you listen, answer the questions. Then compare your answers with a partner.

1. Why does a city need a good brand?
2. What slogan was used in Amsterdam?
3. Where was the slogan used?
4. What was the result?

Listening for Signpost Phrases in a Lecture

LEARN

In a lecture, a speaker will often use signpost phrases to introduce a new topic, to emphasize a main point, or to give an example. Listen for these phrases so that you will know when new or important information is coming up. Here are some common signpost phrases.

To introduce the topic:	Today I'm going to talk about / look at … Let's begin / start with …
To move on to a new topic:	Now, … OK. So … Now let's talk about / look at / move on to …
To give an example:	For example, …
To emphasize a point:	One important point is … In fact, …
To add a point:	And another thing, … Also, …

APPLY

A. Listen to the lecture again. Listen for the signpost phrases that the speaker uses. Which ones do you hear? Circle them in the chart above.

B. Listen to the lecture again. Note the missing information after each of the signpost phrases in bold. (Make notes. You do not need to write the exact words.)

1. Good morning. **Today I'm going to talk about** *a key concept in mktg*____.

2. **In fact,** _____.

3. **For example, let's look at** _____.

4. **Now, let's talk about …** _____.

5. Well, **one important point is** _____.

6. **Also,** _____.

7. **For example,** _____.

C. Compare your answers with a partner. Then take turns summarizing the lecture. Use your notes to guide you.

Vocabulary Activities

A. In the paragraph below, cross out the word or phrase with a different meaning from the other two choices. Use a dictionary to help you understand new words.

When you are designing a logo for a company, it's important to get the details just right. Even a 1. (*large / minor / small*) change can have a big impact. The 2. (*aim / result / goal*) of a good logo is to communicate a clear and simple message and to 3. (*emphasize / highlight / remember*) the important things about the product. When a company redesigns a well-known logo, consumer reaction is not always 4. (*good / negative / positive*), so it's important to test the idea carefully before making a change. 5. (A *lot of / minority of / small number of*) people may complain, but, as the designer, you hope that most people will like it!

B. Some of the target words have multiple meanings. For the target words below, match the dictionary definitions on the left with the example sentences on the right.

positive (adjective)

Definitions	**Example Sentences**
_b_ 1. sure or definite	a. The test results were positive.
___ 2. confident that something good will happen	b. Are you positive that you locked the door?
___ 3. effective, good, or useful	c. I think I will get the job. I feel very positive about my interview.
___ 4. not negative (in math or science)	d. The advertising campaign had a positive effect.

minor (adjective, noun)

Definitions	**Example Sentences**
___ 1. not very large, important, or serious	a. He's studying French with a minor in art history.
___ 2. a person who is under the age at which you legally become an adult	b. Don't worry about it. It's only a minor problem.
___ 3. a second subject that you study in college	c. If you are a minor, your parent must sign this document.

C. Complete the sentences, using *minor* and one of the words from the box.

character	damage	details	illness	injury

1. The president is not at work today. He is suffering from a ___minor illness___ .

2. There was some _____ to the car after the accident.

3. The soccer player was hurt, but it was only a _____ .

4. The actor first played a _____ in a Shakespeare play.

5. Just give us the important information. Don't tell us all the _____ .

D. To *highlight* something means to give it special attention, or to emphasize it. Imagine you are designing an advertisement for each of the following products and services. Work with a partner. Share what features you would highlight for each one.

1. a laptop computer *I would highlight that it's fast and lightweight.*
2. a luxury car
3. a new type of laundry detergent
4. an online grocery delivery service
5. a dry-cleaning service

E. Look at the different uses of the word *positive* below. Work with a partner. Discuss what the word means in the context of each sentence.

1. I really believe in positive thinking.
   Positive thinking means being optimistic and believing that the future will be good.
2. My son's teacher is having a positive influence on him.
3. It's important to make a positive impression at a job interview.
4. The customers had a positive reaction to the new website design.

F. A *goal* is a purpose or aim, something you hope to achieve. Work with a partner to discuss and answer the questions.

1. What is the goal of each of the following?

   a student   a professional athlete   a doctor   an advertisement

2. What are your goals …

   for this week?   for this semester?   for this year?   for the next few years?

About the Topic

Company logos are everywhere nowadays. A good logo has to communicate the company's message in one simple, recognizable image. However, it can be difficult to design a good logo; in fact, some logos are more successful than others.

Before You Watch

Read these questions. Discuss your answers in a small group.

1. What company logos do you see every day? Where do you see them?

2. What logos do you like and why?

3. What do you think makes a good logo?

Watch

Read the Listen for Main Ideas activity below. Go online to watch a presentation on logo design.

Listen for Main Ideas

Answer the questions below. Then compare your answers with a partner.

1. What are the four features of a good logo that the speaker mentions?

instantly recognizable

_____

_____

_____

2. What does each logo suggest? Match the company name with what the logo suggests.

____ Wendy's	a. positive and friendly mood
____ Twitter	b. speed
____ Nike	c. an old-fashioned company

SPEAKING SKILL Using Signpost Phrases in a Short Presentation

LEARN

In the first part of this unit, you learned about signpost phrases that help you identify the main parts of a lecture. In this video, the speaker uses another type of signposting. He tells you in advance how many points he will make, and he numbers the points as he makes them. If you use this strategy, it will make your presentations clearer and easier to understand. Look at the example phrases on page 81.

I'm going to talk about / describe three / four points / reasons / ways ...

Firstly, First of all, ...
The first example / point / reason / way is ...

Secondly, Next, ...
The second point / reason / way is ...
Another example / point / reason / way is ...

Finally ...
The final example / point / reason / way is ...

APPLY

A. Go online and watch the first part of the video again. Circle the signpost phrases the speaker uses in the box above. Compare your answers with a partner.

B. Continue working with your partner. Choose one of the topics below. Complete the introduction and write signpost phrases. Then complete the outline by adding examples and information from your own experience.

1. Three reasons that people play sports

   Introduction: _I'm going to talk about ..._ .

   1. The first reason _____

   2. _____

   3. _____

2. Three ways to save money

   Introduction: _I'm going to explain ..._ .

   1. The first way _____

   2. _____

   3. _____

C. Give a short presentation (one to two minutes) to your partner on the topic you chose. Use the signpost phrases to help make the structure of your presentation clear. Listen for your partner's use of signpost phrases.

PRONUNCIATION SKILL — Sequence Words and Phrases

LEARN

Sequence words and phrases put information in order for the listener. They are signal words that speakers use in presentations and that you can use in conversations, too.

A. Go online to listen to the following examples of sequence words and phrases.

First of all / Secondly / Thirdly	Next
Last	Then
Finally	Later
To begin with	Meanwhile
Before that	After that

B. Sequence words and phrases make up a chunk, or a meaningful word or group of words in a sentence. Remember that after a chunk, you pause (|). Listen to the sentences below.

First, | my goal was to win the logo design contest on my own.
Then, | I decided that it was better to work with a team.

C. With sequence words, the intonation, or the rise and fall of your voice, rises at the beginning of the sentence. Then, at the end of the sentence, the intonation falls. Listen to the sentences.

Later, | I was positive I had made the right decision since we won.

Finally, | the highlight of the experience was getting to see our logo in print.

APPLY

A. Listen to the sentences. Draw a line (|) to show a pause after a sequence word or phrase. Then draw arrows showing rising or falling intonation above the sequence words and phrases and at the end of the statement. Compare your answers with a partner.

1. First of all, | it is important for us to discuss the trip.

2. Secondly, we should talk about marketing feedback.

3. Then, let's break into small groups to talk about the slogan.

4. Next, we can discuss the minor details.

5. Finally, I want to acknowledge all of your hard work.

B. Say the sentences in activity A on page 82 with the correct pausing and intonation.

C. With a partner, use sequence words to give instructions. Tell how you make your favorite meal, send a text message, or play a sport, for example. Use correct pausing and intonation.

> A: To begin with, | boil water. Next, | pour in the pasta. After that, | start chopping up vegetables.

D. With a partner, draw a timeline to describe a period of your life. Present the timeline. Use sequence words and phrases to put the information in order. Use the sentence starters below to describe the timeline. Use correct pausing and intonation.

> A: First, | I moved here when I was 22 years old. Then, | I found a job as a waitress. Meanwhile, | I started to take English classes ...

I started to ...

I found a job ...

I moved ...

I graduated ...

I decided to ...

I wanted to ...

End of Unit Task

In this unit, you learned the importance of branding, slogans, and logo design. You also learned how to listen for and use signpost phrases in a presentation. You will practice this skill by planning and presenting a campaign, which you will then revise based on group feedback.

A. Imagine that you have been asked to plan a campaign to attract visitors to a town or city you know well. Consider the following questions, and make notes of your ideas.

1. Why do people visit the town? What cultural attractions are there?

2. What other activities can people do there? What about sports? Outdoor activities? Museums? Shopping?

3. What kind of public events, such as concerts or festivals, might help to bring visitors to the town?

4. How and where could you advertise the town? Is there a slogan or a logo you could use?

B. Work in small groups. Compare your notes. Add ideas from other students.

C. Plan a group presentation to present your campaign. Each person should deliver part of the presentation. Remember to use the phrases in the box below in your speech.

Today I'm going to talk about / look at ...	I'm going to talk about / describe three / four points / reasons / ways ...
Right. Let's begin with ...	First of all, ...
Now, ...	The first point / reason / way is ...
OK. So ...	Secondly, Next, ...
Now let's talk about / look at ...	The second point / reason / way is ...
For example, ...	Another point / reason / way is ...
One important point is ...	Finally, ...
In fact, ...	The final point / reason / way is ...
And another thing, ...	
Also, ...	

D. Practice the presentation in your group. Listen to your classmates and take notes. Then give feedback. Was the information clearly presented? Did your classmates use signpost phrases? Did this help you understand the main points?

E. Revise your presentation, incorporating the feedback. Then give a group presentation to the class. Each person should speak for two to three minutes.

Self-Assessment		
Yes	**No**	
☐	☐	I can listen for and use signpost phrases.
☐	☐	I successfully made notes on my partners' presentations.
☐	☐	I revised my presentation according to feedback.
☐	☐	I can use correct intonation for sequence words and phrases.
☐	☐	I can correctly use the target vocabulary words from the unit.

Discussion Questions

With a partner or in a small group, discuss the following questions.

1. What slogans do you know? Do you think they are effective or not?

2. What are some logos that you like? Why are they appealing?

3. What is more important, a company's product or its logo and slogan?

UNIT 8

Artistic Vision

In this unit, you will

> learn about art and a particular artist.
> increase your understanding of the target academic words for this unit.

LISTENING AND SPEAKING SKILLS

> Summarizing after You Listen
> Participating in Class Discussions
> **PRONUNCIATION** Sentence Focus and New Information

Self-Assessment

Think about how well you know each target word, and check (✓) the appropriate column. I have…

TARGET WORDS	never seen this word before.	heard or seen the word but am not sure what it means.	heard or seen the word and understand what it means.	used the word confidently in *either* speaking or writing.
AWL				
🔑 available				
🔑 define				
🔑 depress				
🔑 display				
🔑 media				
🔑 symbol				
🔑 temporary				
🔑 vision				

🔑 Oxford 3000™ keywords

Vocabulary Activities

A. Read the sentences. Cross out the word or phrase in parentheses with a different meaning from the other two choices. Use a dictionary to help you understand new words. Compare answers with a partner.

1. Is our art professor (*available* / *free* / ~~*busy*~~) after class?
2. He needs glasses if he doesn't have good (*eyesight* / *vision* / *hearing*).
3. If you feel (*happy* / *sad* / *depressed*), you should talk to a friend.
4. That artist is (*interested in* / *defined by* / *known for*) her use of color.
5. He has a(n) (*image* / *vision* / *word*) in his head of what he wants to create.
6. Are you (*free* / *working* / *available*) after 4:00 p.m.?
7. Please give (*an explanation* / *a definition* / *the pronunciation*) of this word.

Word Form Chart			
Noun	**Verb**	**Adjective**	**Adverb**
availability	_____	available unavailable	_____
definition	define	_____	_____
depression	depress	depressed	depressing
vision	_____	_____	_____

B. Write the target word from the Word Form Chart that works best with each of the phrases below. Use the correct form of the word.

1. The country is in an economic / a serious / a deep __*depression*__ .

2. This is a _____ experience / day / song.

3. I have good / excellent / poor / normal _____ .

4. The book is freely / widely / easily _____ .

5. Please give me a clear / a short / an easy _____ .

C. Work with a partner. Discuss the availability of these items or people. Say why each might be available or unavailable.

1. fruits and vegetables during the summer *Various fruits and vegetables are available during the summer, based on their growing season.*
2. hotel rooms in a popular vacation location
3. the latest smartphone
4. an important politician
5. cheap plane tickets

D. Complete the sentences below with the correct form of *depress*. Then work with a partner to ask and answer the questions.

1. What ___depresses___ you? Why?

2. What kind of weather is most _____ to you?

3. When was the last economic _____ in your country?

4. What do you do to feel better if you're _____?

E. Read the example sentences on the left for *vision*. Match each one to a definition (a–c). Then ask and answer the questions with a partner.

1. What is your vision of a perfect weekend? What is your vision of a perfect vacation?

2. Which leader in your country or the world has or had the best vision?

3. Do you have good vision? Do you wear glasses or contacts?

   a. the ability to see

   b. the ability to make great plans for the future

   c. a picture in your imagination

1. __c__ My vision of a perfect weekend is one where I relax and hang out with friends.

2. ___ _____

3. ___ _____

The word *define* means to say or explain what a word or idea means.

*Can you **define** this word for me?*

*How do you **define** friendship?*

A *definition* is a statement of the meaning of a word, phrase, or idea.

*What is the **definition** of this word?*

*What is your **definition** of happiness?*

CORPUS

F. Discuss the following questions in small groups.

1. What is the definition of a good student? *I think the definition of a good student is someone who studies hard, participates in class, and completes all their work on time.*

2. What qualities define a good employee?

3. What is your definition of success?

4. What is your definition of kindness?

5. What qualities define a good friend?

About the Topic

Artists use shape and color to describe what they see. But what if an artist is blind? John Bramblitt is an unusual artist because he is blind. He uses touch to "see" his subjects. His paintings are very colorful and express a lot of emotion.

Before You Watch

Read these questions. Discuss your answers in a small group.

1. Have you ever drawn or painted a picture? What are the steps in the process of making a painting?

2. Do you know any artists? Describe them. What qualities are important to be a good artist?

3. What would be some challenges for an artist who can't see?

Watch

Read the Listen for Main Ideas activity below. Go online to watch John Bramblitt talk about his work and experience as an artist who is blind.

Listen for Main Ideas

Mark each sentence as *T* (true) or F (false). Work with a partner. Restate false sentences to make them correct.

_F_ 1. John Bramblitt has always been blind.

___ 2. He uses his fingers to feel the paint and mix colors.

___ 3. He met his wife before he was blind, so he knows what she looks like.

___ 4. He teaches children his techniques for painting.

___ 5. He is very positive about the future.

LISTENING SKILL Summarizing after You Listen

LEARN

Summarizing means restating the main points of what you hear in a few sentences. Summarizing can help you remember what you've heard and show that you've understood. Use these guidelines to make a summary after you listen.

1. Make notes.

2. Re-read your notes and choose the main points.

3. Write the main points in a paragraph. Don't include minor details.

A. Go online to watch the first part of the video again. Read the notes and then read the summary. How are they different? Which one includes minor details? Discuss your answers with a partner.

> NOTES
> John Bramblitt – artist, paints colorful paintings with emotion
> became blind – at 30 (9 yrs ago), from epilepsy
> was very depressed (black, felt like he was in a hole)
> taught himself to paint to get over depression
>
>
> SUMMARY
> John Bramblitt is an artist who is blind. He became blind as an adult. He taught himself to paint as a way to get over his depression about becoming blind.

APPLY

A. Go online to watch the second part of the video again. Read the two summaries below. Which one is better? Why?

1. He mixes colors by feeling the different textures of the paint. Some colors are thick and some are thin. He uses his fingers to outline and fill in a painting. He uses his fingers to touch people and "see" them. Then he can paint portraits of them.

2. He mixes colors by feeling the paint. He outlines and paints with his fingers. For portraits, he uses his fingers to "see" the people he paints.

B. Go online to watch the rest of the video. Complete the following summary for that section.

People are starting to notice his art. He goes to museums and schools to

_____ . His view of the future is _____ .

C. Work in small groups. Take turns summarizing each section of the video. Try to do this without looking at your notes.

Vocabulary Activities

A. Using the target words in the box below, complete the paragraph. Be sure to use the correct form and tense of each word.

display	media	symbolize	temporary

The art collection on ____*display*____ at the Wren Library is very interesting. It
(1. show)

is abstract art, but it is not too difficult to understand. You can see what the

art _____ easily. It is a good exhibit for people who think they don't
(2. represents)

like abstract art. The exhibit is _____; it ends next week. Despite a
(3. short)

lack of _____ exposure, the exhibit has been very popular.
(4. newspapers, etc.)

Word Form Chart			
Noun	**Verb**	**Adjective**	**Adverb**
display	display	displayed	_____
media	_____	_____	_____
symbol	symbolize	symbolic	symbolically

B. Use the target words from the Word Form Chart to complete the sentences below. Be sure to use the correct form of each word.

1. The new art exhibit at the museum was discussed in the ____*media*____.

2. What does this sculpture _____? I don't know what it means.

3. There are some new paintings on _____ at the museum.

C. Complete the sentences with a target word and its collocation.

on display	temporary exhibit	media attention	powerful symbol

1. Many people feel that art can be a ____*powerful symbol*____ for many things.

2. You should go see the _____ at the museum soon.

3. There are some new paintings _____ at the museum.

4. The exhibit at the museum has received a lot of _____. It's been in the news online and on TV.

D. The word *media* describes television, newspapers, and radio as a means of communication. List different types of media within each category. Then compare answers with a partner. See if you can add any more.

1. print media: *newspapers*   2. TV: 3. radio:

E. Work with a partner. Use *symbol* or *symbolizes* to talk about the pictures below. Can you think of any more symbols? *A heart is a symbol for love.*

The word *display* has several different meanings:

1. an act of showing something happening, to entertain:

   *a fireworks **display***

2. an arrangement of things to be seen in a public place:

   *a **display** of new products*

3. behavior that shows a particular feeling or quality:

   *a **display** of aggression*

CORPUS

F. Answer the questions and discuss them in small groups.

1. Where might you see a display of aggression? *You might see a display of aggression between athletes at a sports event.*

2. When and where is the last time you saw a fireworks display?

3. What is something you are proud to display in your home or office?

G. Answer and discuss the questions in small groups.

1. Which type of media gives you the most information? *Newspapers, I think.*

2. Which type of media talks about celebrities the most?

3. Which type of media is fastest and most convenient?

H. Which of these things are temporary? Which are not? Compare your answers in small groups. Be prepared to explain your answer.

a cold or the flu *A cold or the flu is temporary because they usually only last about a week.*

a headache   a rainy day

a forest   an art exhibit

an ocean   a song

About the Topic

Students in art classes usually study various types of art. It is also typical for them to visit different museums and art exhibits. As part of the class, students may be required to give a presentation on some aspect of art.

Before You Listen

Read these questions. Discuss your answers in a small group.

1. Have you been to an art museum? Did you enjoy it? Why or why not?
2. What kind of art do you like: paintings, photography, sculpture?
3. Is art only for enjoyment or should it have other purposes such as making people think about social problems? What is your opinion?

Listen

Read the Listen for Main Ideas activity below. Go online to listen to four students discussing a project for their art class.

Listen for Main Ideas

Think about the answer for each question. Then compare answers with a partner.

1. Do the students have a choice of topics for the presentation?
2. What is the first topic they discuss for the presentation?
3. Do they all agree on the first topic?
4. Is the second topic they discuss related to photography or painting?
5. Do they all agree on the second topic?

SPEAKING SKILL   Participating in Class Discussions

LEARN

It can be difficult to participate in class discussions in a second language. Topics can change quickly and often, and the language can be unpredictable. You also need to take turns speaking. Here are some suggestions.

1. First, respond or react to what the previous speaker said: agree, disagree, or add a comment or suggestion. Then make your point.
2. Interrupt by asking, *May I say something?* You may need to wait for a pause in the conversation before you speak.
3. Ask other people for their opinions. You can say, *What do you think?*
4. Make sure you participate, but don't dominate the conversation.

A. Look at these examples from the conversation. Which of the suggestions in the box on page 92 is each one an example of? Write the number next to the example.

_1_ 1. That sounds good.

___ 2. Maybe we could consider that idea …

___ 3. Do you have any other ideas?

___ 4. What do you think, Karla?

APPLY

A. Go online to listen to four different parts of the conversation. Which suggestions in the box are used in each one? List all that apply, and explain what the speaker does.

1. ___1___ *The speaker responds and agrees with the previous speaker. He adds*

a suggestion.

2. _____

3. _____

4. _____

B. Work in small groups. Look at the question below, and discuss it. During the discussion, try to use each of the class discussion suggestions. If possible, record your conversation.

To learn about art, is it better to visit museums or actually make art (for example, draw or paint)? Why?

C. After you finish, discuss your conversation. If you recorded your conversation, listen to it. Which of the suggestions did you use? Did everyone participate in the conversation? Why or why not?

LEARN

Every sentence has stressed words, or *focus words*. They are usually the content words. You can also stress words to introduce new information.

Remember that content words are the main verbs, nouns, adjectives, adverbs, negatives, and question words in a sentence. They receive the stress and are pronounced fully and completely. Function words do not receive stress. They include articles, short conjunctions, prepositions, pronouns, and auxiliary verbs.

A. Go online to listen to the sentences. Notice the content words in pink.

1. The art exhibit is new.

2. Where did you find the photograph?

In Unit 7, you learned that a chunk is a meaningful group of words in a sentence. Longer sentences have more than one chunk. After a chunk, we pause.

B. Listen to the sentences below. Notice the chunks separated by pauses (|). Notice the content words in pink.

1. Even though he's blind, | John Bramblitt still paints, | using his fingers.

2. The collections in the museum | represent works | from many different artists.

Each chunk has a stressed *focus word*, or the most important word in the chunk. This is usually the last content word and the easiest word to hear. New information is stressed. Old information is unstressed.

C. Go online to listen to the conversation. Notice the focus words and new information in pink.

A: I thought the paintings were beautiful.

B: Which paintings? The ones in the new museum?

A: Yes, in the latest exhibit.

B: Is it still running?

APPLY

A. With a partner, say the conversation in Learn, activity C. Stress the focus words to show the new information.

B. Research a painting that you like. Find out who painted it, when they painted it, and where the artist lived. You can tell your partner why you like the painting, too. Have this information near you on a laptop or written down. Your partner will ask you questions about it. Stress the focus words and the new information.

> A: This is my favorite **painting**.
>
> B: Who **painted** it?
>
> A: The artist **Picasso**.
>
> B: The one who painted **"Guernica"**?
>
> A: **Yes!** I really like his **style**.
>
> B: Let me see the picture. **When** did Picasso paint this?
>
> A: It was **early** in his career. He painted it in **1903**.

End of Unit Task

In this unit, you learned how to summarize after you listen, and you practiced participating in class discussions. You will review these skills by listening to and summarizing another conversation. Then, you will participate in a class discussion.

A. Go online to listen to the conversation. What is the main topic: a plan for an art class for children, college students, or adults?

B. Listen again. Write a short summary of the conversation. Compare your summary with a partner. How similar are the summaries?

C. You are going to plan an art class. First, choose a type of class from the list below. Then, use the questions to help you plan. You can also use your own ideas.

- a one-day class for college students
- an after-school class for high school students
- an evening class for working adults

1. What kind of art will students study?
2. Will students create art in the class (for example, paint or draw), or just study art and visit museums?
3. Will the class be held online, in a classroom, in a museum, or some combination of these?

D. Work in small groups. Discuss your ideas to make a plan for the art class. Make sure you use the suggestions below to participate in the group discussion.

> 1. First, respond or react to what the previous speaker said: agree, disagree, or add a comment or suggestion. Then make your point.
> 2. Interrupt by asking, *May I say something?* You may need to wait for a pause in the conversation before you speak.
> 3. Ask other people for their opinions. You can say, *What do you think?*
> 4. Make sure you participate, but don't dominate the conversation.

E. After you finish your discussion, summarize your plan for the art class. Also, check whether everyone participated in the discussion. Did you use some of the suggestions from the box above?

F. Compare your summaries with other groups. How similar or different are your plans for the art class?

Self-Assessment		
Yes	**No**	
☐	☐	I can summarize after listening.
☐	☐	I successfully practiced participating in class discussions.
☐	☐	I can hear stress on focus words and new information in a sentence.
☐	☐	I can stress focus words and new information when speaking.
☐	☐	I can correctly use the target vocabulary words from the unit.

Discussion Questions

With a partner or in a small group, discuss the following questions.

1. Have you ever taken an art class? What did you study or create?
2. What kind of media do you use to get news and information?
3. What are some symbols that you think are significant? What about them appeals to you?

UNIT 9

Dynamic Earth

In this unit, you will

> learn about tectonic plates and volcanoes.
> increase your understanding of the target academic words for this unit.

LISTENING AND SPEAKING SKILLS

> Key Terms and Definitions
> Asking for Clarification
> **PRONUNCIATION** Chunking

Self-Assessment

Think about how well you know each target word, and check (✓) the appropriate column. I have…

TARGET WORDS	never seen this word before.	heard or seen the word but am not sure what it means.	heard or seen the word and understand what it means.	used the word confidently in *either* speaking or writing.
AWL				
🔑 appreciate				
🔑 energy				
🔑 predict				
🔑 previous				
🔑 remove				
🔑 role				
🔑 section				
🔑 series				

🔑 Oxford 3000™ keywords

Vocabulary Activities

A. Cross out the word or phrase in parentheses with a different meaning from the other two choices. Use a dictionary to help you understand new words.

Mount St. Helens is a volcano in the western United States that erupted dramatically on May 18, 1980. If you look at pictures of the volcano before and after the eruption, you will 1. (*appreciate / hear / understand*) the enormous 2. (*energy / force / information*) that caused it. After the eruption, the top 3. (*part / section / side*) of the mountain was gone. 4. (*Before this / Previously / Fortunately*), this area had been a beautiful forest, but now it is covered with ash.

B. Some words have multiple meanings. Match the dictionary definitions on the left with the example sentences on the right.

> appreciate

Definitions

__c__ 1. to recognize the good qualities of something

____ 2. to understand that something is true

____ 3. to be grateful for something or someone

Example Sentences

a. If you look at the statistics, you will appreciate the problem.

b. Thank you. I really appreciate your help.

c. The artist's work was not appreciated until after she died.

C. Write 1, 2, or 3 depending on the meaning of *appreciate* in each sentence.

__3__ 1. Could you please give me a ride? I'd appreciate it.

____ 2. Later in life, I appreciated my mother's good advice.

____ 3. We didn't appreciate how long the project would take.

____ 4. It's important to teach children to appreciate music.

____ 5. We would appreciate your feedback.

Word Form Chart			
Noun	**Verb**	**Adjective**	**Adverb**
appreciation	appreciate	(un)appreciated	appreciably
energy	_____	energetic	energetically
_____	_____	previous	previously

D. Using the target words in the Word Form Chart on page 98, complete these sentences. Be sure to use the correct form and tense of each word.

1. Plants use ____energy____ from the sun to grow.

2. Thank you so much for your help. I really _____ it.

3. It's difficult to find a job if you don't have _____ experience.

4. The parents' hard work is often _____ by their children.

5. I recognized George because we had met _____.

6. Vera is such a(n) _____ person. She never stops moving!

7. The students gave the teacher a gift to show their _____.

Energy is the ability to put effort and enthusiasm into an activity. The adjective is *energetic*.

> I'm feeling very tired and I don't have any **energy**.

> The children are so **energetic**! They can play for hours.

Energy is also used to describe power that comes from electricity, gas, coal, etc.

> The house is heated by solar **energy**.

CORPUS

E. Discuss the following questions with a partner.

1. Are you an energetic person? Why or why not?
2. When do you feel most energetic?
3. If you're feeling tired, what do you do to boost your energy?
4. What different kinds of energy (electric, gas, solar, etc.) are used in your home or school?

F. Discuss the questions with a partner. Use the word *previous* in your answer.

1. What kinds of jobs require previous experience? What kinds do not? *A job as a chef requires previous experience.*
2. Do you know the previous residents of your house or apartment?
3. How is your generation different from previous generations?
4. What kind of people want to beat a previous record?

A *section* is any of the parts into which something (a book, a chapter, a class, etc.) can be divided.

> Please read the **section** on earthquakes in your textbook.

> This class, English 110, has three **sections**.

CORPUS

G. Work with a partner. Discuss how each of the items below can be divided into sections.

In a library, there's a children's section and a reference section.

a library   an orchestra   your country or your city

a newspaper   a map   this unit

a restaurant

About the Topic

The surface of the Earth is made of huge sections called tectonic plates. These plates fit together like a jigsaw puzzle. Geologists believe that the plates were once joined together, and that over time they split apart.

Before You Watch

Read these questions. Discuss your answers in a small group.

1. What is geology? What does a geologist study?

2. Would you like to be a geologist? Why or why not?

3. What kinds of places are interesting for geologists and why?

Watch

Read the Listen for Main Ideas activity below. Go online to watch the video about plate boundaries and how the continents were formed.

Listen for Main Ideas

Choose the correct answer to complete the statements from the video.

1. The rock face in Iceland is interesting because ___.

   a. it is made of a special type of rock

   (b.) it is part of a boundary between two sections of the Earth

2. The underwater scene shows ___.

   a. the gap between the continents of Europe and North America

   b. a place where warm water comes out of the Earth

3. According to the video, millions of years ago, the continents were ___.

   a. joined together

   b. under water

4. According to the video, ___ caused the continents to move apart.

   a. an enormous earthquake

   b. heat from the center of the Earth

LEARN

In a lecture, speakers sometimes introduce terms that are important to your understanding of the topic. They often define these terms during the lecture. As you listen, it's important to identify these words and write them down. Speakers highlight them in different ways.

- They say the words more loudly and slowly.
- They repeat the words.
- They write the words on the board.
- They define the words, using expressions such as:
  This is called … / This is known as … / We call this …

APPLY

A. Watch the video again. Check (✓) the four key terms that are introduced. Compare your answers with a partner.

____ the Earth's surface

____ tectonic plates

____ the plate boundary

____ the Mid-Atlantic Ridge

____ heat inside the Earth

____ the Earth's core

____ hot rock

B. Watch the video again. Make a note of what each of the four terms means. Which of the techniques from the box above does the speaker use?

C. Define one of the terms. See if your partner can name it.

> A: The Earth is divided into sections. What are they called?
>
> B: Tectonic plates.

Vocabulary Activities

Word Form Chart			
Noun	**Verb**	**Adjective**	**Adverb**
prediction	predict	predictable unpredictable	predictably unpredictably
removal	remove	removable	_____

A. Complete the sentences below with the correct form of *predict* or *remove.*

1. The weather channel ___predicted___ that it will rain today. But the _____ are not always accurate!

2. Some volcanoes are quite _____; they can erupt at any time. Scientists can never _____ exactly when that will be.

3. Clean the area with soap to _____ the dirt.

4. The hood of my jacket is _____. I can take it off when the weather is warm.

5. The city is responsible for the _____ of garbage in my town.

B. Choose the best definition for the word in bold in each sentence.

_a_ 1. The actress who played the **role** of Juliet was very good.

    a. a part in a play or movie

    b. the function of something in a situation

____ 2. Parents play an important **role** in their children's education.

    a. a part in a play or movie

    b. the function of something in a situation

____ 3. Scientists have researched the **role** of volcanoes in climate change.

    a. a part in a play or movie

    b. the function of something in a situation

____ 4. The police studied the **series** of events leading to the accident.

    a. a number of things that come one after another and are connected

    b. a set of TV or radio shows that have the same characters

____ 5. That comedy **series** has been popular for many years.

    a. a number of events that come one after another and are connected

    b. a set of TV or radio shows that have the same characters

____ 6. Our team won a **series** of important games, and went on to win the finals.

    a. a number of things that come one after another and are connected

    b. a set of TV or radio shows that have the same characters

A *role* is the function of something in a situation. If something plays a role in a situation, it has an effect on that situation.

> *Volcanoes play a **role** in the Earth's climate.*

> *Our management style plays an important **role** in our company's success.*

CORPUS

C. Work with a partner. Say which of the factors on the left play a role in the life events on the right, and how.

> *The weather plays a role in planning a vacation because when you go on vacation you usually want good weather.*

Factors	Life events
the weather	choosing a career
being able to speak English	getting a good job
your study habits	planning a vacation
money	succeeding in school
your hobbies and interests	determining where to live
your family	

D. To *remove* is to take something or someone away or off. Complete the sentences by using a word or expression from each box.

> *When we enter the house, we always remove our shoes.*

1. When we enter the house, we always remove
2. The doctor removed
3. This detergent will remove
4. The government voted to remove
5. Volunteers are working to remove

the senator	from our public parks.
food stains	from my hand.
our shoes.	_____
a piece of metal	from your clothes.
trash	from office.

E. Which of the following can you predict? How?

> *You can predict the weather with satellites or by looking at the sky.*

the weather	an earthquake
your exam results	when prices will go up
what team will win a game	what song or movie will be popular

About the Topic

Most of the world's volcanoes are located along the Ring of Fire, which circles the Pacific Ocean. Along this ring, several tectonic plates meet. Most volcanoes are caused when one tectonic plate moves below another.

Before You Listen

Read these questions. Discuss your answers in a small group.

1. Have you ever seen an active volcano? Where and when?

2. Can you name any well-known volcanoes? Which ones?

3. What kind of damage is caused by a volcanic eruption?

Listen

Read the Listen for Main Ideas activity below. Go online to listen to an explanation of what happens when a volcano erupts.

Listen for Main Ideas

Number the topics 1–5 in the order that they are discussed. Compare your answers with a partner.

____ Predicting volcanoes

____ Tectonic plates

____ The effects of a volcanic eruption

____ The Ring of Fire

____ How volcanoes happen

| SPEAKING SKILL | Asking for Clarification |

LEARN

When you don't understand something, or you miss an important piece of information in a lecture or a study group, you need to ask the speaker to clarify or repeat the information. Below are some expressions that you can use to ask for clarification.

Asking for clarification
May I ask a question?
(I'm sorry.) I (still) don't understand.
I didn't understand the part about ...
Could you please repeat that?
Could you please explain that?
Could you give us an example?
Do you mean ... ?

APPLY

A. Listen to the conversation again and circle the expressions in the box on page 104 that the students use to ask for clarification. Compare your answers with a partner.

B. Choose one of the descriptions A–C below. (<u>Do not</u> read the other descriptions.) Read the one you chose carefully. Make sure that you understand and can pronounce the underlined words. Use a dictionary if necessary.

A: There are three kinds of volcanoes: <u>active</u>, <u>dormant</u>, and <u>extinct</u>. An active volcano erupts regularly. A dormant volcano has erupted in the past but is now quiet. An extinct volcano is unlikely to erupt again. There are around <u>1,500</u> active volcanoes in the world.

B: When a volcano erupts, it sends <u>ash</u>, <u>gas</u>, and <u>magma</u> into the air. On the ground, a volcanic eruption can also cause <u>earthquakes</u>, <u>floods</u>, and <u>tsunamis</u>, and destroy the landscape for miles around.

C: The world's largest active volcano is <u>Mauna Loa</u>, which is located in <u>Hawaii</u>. Mauna Loa is <u>13,677</u> feet above sea level. From its base below sea level to its peak, it is higher than Mount Everest.

C. Work with two other students who chose different descriptions. Read your description to your classmates. Then listen and take notes on your classmates' descriptions. Ask for repetition and clarification when necessary. Use the expressions in the box on page 104.

D. Compare your notes with the original description. Did you note the information accurately?

PRONUNCIATION SKILL   Chunking

LEARN

In Units 7 and 8, you learned that a chunk is a meaningful word or group of words in a sentence. There are many different examples of chunking in spoken speech. Chunks can have their own intonation, which is the rise and fall of speech.

When you list a series of items, each item is one chunk. Items can be single words or phrases. Pause (|) after each item. Use rising intonation after each item until the final item. Use falling intonation on the final item.

 A. Go online to listen to the following sentences.

1. It runs along the ocean floor, | rises above the sea, | and cuts a sharp line.

2. It's an area that runs from New Zealand | through Indonesia, | Japan, | Alaska, | and down the west coast of North America.

When words are spelled out loud, the letters are usually chunked in groups of two, three, or four. Use rising intonation on each chunk except the last one, and insert a pause (|) after each item.

 B. Go online to listen to the examples.

1. *Appreciate* is spelled A-P-P | R-E-C | I-A-T-E.

2. *Tectonic* is spelled T-E-C | T-O-N | I-C.

When long sets of numbers are said out loud, these are also usually chunked in groups of two, three, or four numbers. Use rising intonation on each chunk except the last one, and insert a pause (|) after each item.

 C. Go online to listen to the examples.

1. My phone number is 617 | 555 | 0076.

2. The password is 899 | 25 | 66.

APPLY

 A. Go online to listen to the sentences. Draw lines showing pauses. Then draw arrows showing the appropriate intonation above the items.

1. The lower plate becomes hot, | the rock melts, | and the melted rock is pushed up to the Earth's surface.

2. Tectonic plates carry entire continents, extend far under the sea, and meet at the plate boundary.

3. Scientists try to predict earthquakes, volcanoes, and other forces of nature.

B. Listen to the words and numbers. Draw lines showing where the speaker pauses. Then draw arrows above the items showing the intonation that you hear for each part.

1. P-R-E | -V-I | -O-U-S
2. E-A-R-T-H-Q-U-A-K-E
3. S-E-C-T-I-O-N
4. E-R-U-P-T-I-O-N

5. 2 0 2 8 2
6. 1 1 1 5 5 2 8 9
7. 8 0 0 2 9 6 7 4 3 1

C. Say the sentences in Apply, activity A. Use the correct intonation and pause where appropriate.

D. Work with a partner. Quiz each other on how to spell difficult words. Use appropriate rising and falling intonation and pausing.

A: Spell continent.
B: C-O-N | T-I-N | E-N-T

E. With a partner, talk about what you do on a typical day or on the weekend. List at least three things or activities. Use appropriate rising and falling intonation and pausing.

A: What do you do on Saturdays?
B: I clean the house, | do my laundry, | and study. What do you do?
A: I make dinner for the week. I cook pasta, | rice, | and meat.

End of Unit Task

In this unit, you learned to identify key terms and definitions in a lecture. You also learned how to ask for clarification when there is something that you don't understand. Review these skills by choosing a topic that you know well, and explaining it to your classmates.

A. Think of a subject you are an expert in and can talk about for three minutes. Read the list of suggestions below, or use your own idea.

something you're studying in another class	an event in history
the rules of a game or sport that you know well	a news story
how you play a favorite computer or video game	a place you've visited

B. Organize your talk into three to five parts. Decide what you will say in each part. Include some key terms and definitions in your talk.

C. Work in small groups. Take turns speaking about your topic. Listen to your classmates. Take notes on the main points and key terms from their talks. Ask for clarification when necessary. Use the expressions in the box below.

Asking for clarification	
May I ask a question?	Could you please explain that?
(I'm sorry.) I (still) don't understand.	Could you give us an example?
I didn't understand the part about …	Do you mean … ?
Could you please repeat that?	

D. Compare your notes with your classmates. Decide together on the main points and key terms. Then confirm your decision with the speaker.

Self-Assessment		
Yes	**No**	
☐	☐	I can identify key terms and definitions when listening.
☐	☐	I can ask for clarification when I do not understand.
☐	☐	I was able to clarify some points for my classmates.
☐	☐	I understand pausing and intonation with chunking when listening and speaking.
☐	☐	I can correctly use the target vocabulary words from the unit.

Discussion Questions

With a partner or in a small group, discuss the following questions.

1. Some people visit active volcanoes with adventure tourism vacations. Would you go on a trip like this? Why or why not?

2. Imagine you have an opportunity to study overseas in a country that is known to have earthquakes. Would you go? Why or why not?

3. What are some recent earthquakes you can remember? What media source(s) gave you information about them?

UNIT 10

You Can Make It

In this unit, you will

> learn about the maker movement.
> increase your understanding of the target academic words for this unit.

LISTENING AND SPEAKING SKILLS

> Listening for Supporting Ideas
> Using Sequence Words
> **PRONUNCIATION** Common Reductions

Self-Assessment

Think about how well you know each target word, and check (✓) the appropriate column. I have...

TARGET WORDS	never seen this word before.	heard or seen the word but am not sure what it means.	heard or seen the word and understand what it means.	used the word confidently in *either* speaking or writing.
AWL				
🔑 adult				
🔑 attach				
🔑 culture				
🔑 design				
🔑 draft				
🔑 intelligence				
🔑 job				
🔑 require				

🔑 Oxford 3000™ keywords

Vocabulary Activities

A. Read the sentences. Circle the word or phrase in parentheses that has the same meaning as the underlined word in the sentence. Compare your answers with a partner.

1. A do-it-yourself, or DIY, project <u>requires</u> (*helps / assists / needs*) time.

2. If making things yourself was not part of the <u>culture</u> (*way of life / city / time*) you grew up in, DIY might be difficult for you.

3. You don't need a lot of <u>intelligence</u> (*intellect / thought / care*) for DIY, but you usually do need patience.

B. Complete the Word Form Chart with the correct forms of the target words below. Use a dictionary to check your answers. One word can go in two categories.

adult	culturally	unintelligent	required
culture	intelligence	intelligently	requirement
cultural	intelligent	require	

Word Form Chart			
Noun	**Verb**	**Adjective**	**Adverb**
adult			

C. Using the target words in the Word Form Chart, complete the paragraph. Be sure to use the correct form and tense of each word.

In the past, making things by hand was often ___*required*___ because people
                                                    (1. needed)

couldn't always go to a store and buy things. Children learned by watching

their parents and other _____ make things. As the _____
                         (2. grown-ups)   (3. way of life)

changed, though, people could buy what they wanted at a store. Fewer

people made things by hand. However, DIY is popular again. And you don't

even have to be that _____ to make something yourself. There is a lot
                      (4. smart)

of DIY information on the Internet. The main _____ is taking time
                                               (5. necessity)

to learn.

D. **Work with a partner. Discuss the requirements for each of these activities.**

1. to get a driver's license *The requirements to get a driver's license are to take classes, practice driving, and pass a test.*

2. to get a high school diploma

3. to get into college

4. to borrow a book from the library

5. to take money out of the bank / ATM

6. to get a good grade in this class

E. **Check (✓) which activities are typical for an adult to do. Consider which are not. Discuss your answers with a partner.**

✓ drive a car *It's typical for an adult to drive a car.*

___ rent an apartment

___ get married

___ go to school

___ play with toys

___ go shopping

___ live with parents

___ go to a park

The word *culture* describes the customs, ideas, etc., of a group of people. It also describes achievement in arts and literature.

> The language and **culture** of the Aztecs interest many people.
>
> New York City is a center of **culture** in the U.S.

The adjective form is *cultural*. The adjective form for a person who is well educated and knows a lot about music, art, and literature is *cultured*.

> The city has an active **cultural** life. There are many museums, theaters, and concert halls.
>
> She is very **cultured**. She knows a lot about art, music, and books.

 CORPUS

F. **Work with a partner. Discuss the following questions.**

1. What do you know about the traditional culture of your country? Describe it. *Traditional cultures vary across my country, but some would say hot dogs and baseball are part of our traditional culture.*

2. What city is the cultural center of your state? Why?

3. Who is someone you know that is cultured? Describe him / her.

4. What is a cultural event that you have attended recently? Was it good? Why or why not?

G. Rate these in order (1–8) according to how much intelligence you think is required. 1 = least, 8 = most. Discuss your answers in small groups.

____ designing a house   ____ using a smartphone

____ calculating change   ____ memorizing a list of words

____ speaking two languages   ____ posting on a social networking site

____ finding your way in a new place   ____ memorizing scientific information

About the Topic

The *maker movement* describes people who make objects and products themselves. When you make something yourself, it's called do-it-yourself, or DIY. In the maker movement, people might make electronics, robots, or other technological devices. Often, people in this movement like to share; they share ideas, information, and instructions for making things.

Before You Listen

Read these questions. Discuss your answers in a small group.

1. Do-it-yourself (DIY) projects are popular these days. Why do you think some people like them?

2. Do you know anyone who likes to work on DIY projects? If so, what does he / she make?

3. What can be difficult about DIY projects? What is required?

Listen

Read the Listen for Main Ideas activity below. Go online to listen to an interview with an engineer who talks about the maker movement.

Listen for Main Ideas

Mark each sentence as *T* (true) or *F* (false). Work with a partner. Restate false sentences to make them correct.

_F_ 1. The maker movement is only about building furniture.

____ 2. Sharing information and ideas is part of the philosophy of the movement.

____ 3. Both adults and children are part of the maker movement.

____ 4. Maker Faires are only held in California.

____ 5. Engineers are the main people interested in the movement.

LEARN

A speaker often adds ideas or examples after a main idea to support it. Practicing listening for these supporting ideas will help you better understand the main points a speaker makes.

Look at this example from the interview. Which two ideas support this main point?

Main point: But, the maker movement brings in more technology and engineering.

____ People are building their own electronics at home.

____ People build their own furniture, and so on.

____ For example, your neighbor might be building a robot in his garage.

APPLY

A. Listen to the interview again. As you listen, write down a supporting idea or example for each point. Compare your answers with a partner. Do you have the same answers?

1. Main point: Making something does not have to be expensive.

   There's a tiny computer that only costs $20.

2. Main point: The maker movement is a kind of community.

3. Main point: People make many different things.

4. Main point: Children are part of the movement.

5. Main point: The maker movement is not just for engineers.

B. Work with a partner. Don't look at your notes. Retell the main ideas from the interview. Then quiz your partner. Read a main point from activity A. See if your partner can state the supporting idea. Switch roles.

Vocabulary Activities

A. Complete the paragraph using words from the box. Be sure to use the correct form and tense of each word. One word is used twice.

attach	attachment	design	draft	job

Making a robot at home is a fun, but challenging ____*job*____. You can find
(1. task)

many _____ on the Internet. Be careful, though. Sometimes it looks
(2. plans)

like the work will be easy, but it isn't. If you make a(n) _____ of the
(3. rough version)

project first, you can get an idea of how long the _____ will take.
(4. work)

Finally, make sure you have any extra _____ you might need, and that
(5. parts)

you know how to _____ them correctly.
(6. connect)

B. Some of the target words have multiple meanings. For the target words below, match the dictionary definitions on the left with the example sentences on the right.

design (noun, verb)

Definitions

_b_ 1. a drawing that shows how something may be made

___ 2. to draw plans or make models of something

___ 3. an arrangement of lines and shapes as a decoration

Example Sentences

a. She wants to design the new studio.

b. The architect showed us two designs for a house.

c. That t-shirt has a nice design on it.

draft (noun)

Definitions

___ 1. a piece of writing or drawing that will be changed and improved

___ 2. a flow of cool air that comes into a room

___ 3. a process of choosing players for professional sports teams

Example Sentences

a. Can you please close the window? There's a draft in here.

b. The team chose a talented player in the final draft.

c. I wrote three drafts of the report before I handed it in.

C. The words *design* and *draft* can both be used as nouns or verbs. Write *N* if the word is being used as a noun, and *V* if the word is being used as a verb.

_N_ 1. His teacher asked him to write another draft of the paper.

___ 2. She wants to design clothes as her job.

___ 3. I don't like the design of the house.

___ 4. He is studying interior design.

___ 5. They drafted two new players for the soccer team.

The noun *job* describes the work that you do to earn money.

*My parents told me it was time to get a **job**.*

It can also be used for a task or work that can be paid or unpaid.

*We do lots of **jobs** around the house on weekends.*

CORPUS

D. Choose words from the box to go with *job*. Write questions. Then work with a partner to ask and answer the questions.

big	dream	interesting	unpaid
difficult	ideal	well-paid	

A: What is your ideal job?

B: My ideal job is working in medicine. I'd like to be a doctor or a nurse and help people.

The verb *attach* means to connect something to something else.

*A note was **attached** to the report with a paper clip.*

The adjective *attached (to)* means to like someone or something very much.

*He's become very **attached** to you.*

The noun form is *attachment*.

*There's a strong **attachment** between the child and her parents.*

CORPUS

E. Work with a partner. Look at the list below. Which of these things has physical attachments? Which have emotional attachments? Describe the possible attachments.

1. a computer *A computer has physical attachments. For example, a printer could be attached to a computer.*

2. family members

3. your home

4. an email message

5. your friends

6. your favorite possession

7. a bulletin board

F. Ask and answer the following questions with a partner.

1. What does each of these people design? Which job would you most like to do? Why?

   fashion designer *A fashion designer designs clothes.*

   landscape designer

   software designer

   graphic designer

   interior designer

   jewelry designer

2. Describe something (a building, a machine) that you think is designed well.

3. Describe something that you think is designed poorly. How would you improve the design?

4. What is something you would like to design? Describe it.

About the Topic

A Maker Faire is an event for people who like to design and make things. People show and sell the things they make at a Maker Faire. There are crafts, science and engineering projects, and food and music. The first Maker Faire was held in 2006 in California, in the United States.

Before You Listen

Read these questions. Discuss your answers in a small group.

1. What is something you made or built yourself? (For example, food, furniture, clothing, etc.)

2. What was easy or difficult about making or building it?

3. In general, do you enjoy making or building things? Why or why not?

Listen

Read the Listen for Main Ideas activity below. Go online to listen to the interview with 15-year-old Adriana at a Maker Faire. She talks about what she built and how she built it.

Listen for Main Ideas

Listen to the interview and answer the questions below.

1. Why did Adriana choose a bicycle generator for the project?

2. What was Adriana's problem when she started the project?

3. How did she solve the problem?

4. How long did it take her to do the project?

5. Does she plan to do another project?

Using Sequence Words

LEARN

When you give a presentation, you can use sequence words to tell a story or describe a process. Knowing and using sequence words will help you present information more clearly and help your audience follow your presentation.

Sequence words and expressions	
First, ... To begin / start, ...	After + clause (*After we did that,* ...)
Second, ... Then, ... Next, ...	Finally, ...
Third, ... After that, ...	In the end, ...
When + clause (*When I finished,* ...)	

APPLY

A. Listen to the audio again. Circle the sequence expressions that you hear in the chart. Compare your answers with a partner.

B. Working with the same partner, retell Adriana's process of making the bicycle generator. Use correct sequence words.

C. Look at the example process below with your partner. Put the steps in the correct order. Then add sequence words. Practice describing the process with the sequence words.

Here's the process to make a cup of coffee.

_____ _____ sit down and enjoy your coffee.

_____ _____ add sugar and / or milk. Stir it again.

_____ _____ pour the water over the coffee and stir it.

_____ _____ add coffee to a cup.

_____ _____ heat some water.

D. Work with a new partner. Choose a process from the list below, or come up with your own idea. Make a list of the steps for the process. Then add sequence words to make the process clear.

- Make your favorite snack.
- Post on a social networking site.
- Sign up for a class.
- Enter a user name and password on a website.
- Get a bus pass.
- Email a photo to someone.

E. Work in small groups. Take turns describing your process.

PRONUNCIATION SKILL | Common Reductions

LEARN

In Unit 3, you learned about reduced question forms (such as *Whaddaya* and *Whadija*). You can also reduce common verb phrases in connected speech.

A. Go online to listen to the examples.

Original form	Reduced form	Example
don't know	"dunno"	"dunno" I don't know how to make this by myself.
has to	"hasta"	"hasta" He has to buy new equipment.
have to	"hafta"	"hafta" They have to get different jobs.
want to	"wanna"	"wanna" Do you want to learn more about the community's culture?
wants to	"wansta"	"wansta" Who wants to start a new project?
going to	"gonna"	"gonna" She's going to create her own design.

B. Some reductions combine a verb + *me*. Go online to listen to the examples.

Original form	Reduced form	Example
let me	"lemme"	"lemme" Let me see that.
give me	"gimme"	"gimme" Give me your advice.

APPLY

A. Go online to listen to the sentences. Fill in the original form of the reduction that you hear. Check your answers.

1. He ___*wants to*___ sell his new invention.

2. _____ your opinion about this design.

3. Who's _____ go to the Maker Faire this year?

4. I _____ how to make that, but I'll try.

5. We don't _____, but we _____ stop working on our project.

6. _____ know when you want to go.

7. She _____ buy that special tool online.

B. Say the sentences in Apply, activity A with the correct reduced form.

C. With a partner, talk about a do-it-yourself project that you want to do. Use the reduced question forms in the box below and the reductions from the charts on page 118.

Whaddaya	Whodija	Whendaya	Whydija
Whadija	Wheredaya	Whendija	Howdaya
Whodaya	Wheredija	Whydaya	Howdija

A: Whaddaya wanna make?
B: I wanna make bookshelves for my bedroom.

A: Whaddaya hafta buy first?
B: I hafta get some wood, nails, and paint.

A: Whendaya wanna do this?
B: I dunno, but probably during spring break.

A: Whodija ask to help you?
B: My dad's gonna help me because he's done it before.

End of Unit Task

In this unit, you learned about the maker movement and Maker Faires. You listened for supporting details in an interview and learned how sequencing words can help you organize a presentation. Review these skills by preparing and listening to class presentations.

A. Work with a partner. Choose a process to describe. You can choose a topic from below or use your own idea. You and your partner must agree on one topic, and the topic must be different from the one you described on page 117. Your presentation should be three to five minutes.

How to …

- make your favorite meal or dish

- build a piece of furniture

- repair something on a car (or other machine)

- install a new program on your computer

- change the ink in your printer

- make a piece of clothing

- set the table for a formal dinner and / or prepare for a party

B. Outline and make notes of your ideas with your partner. Think carefully about all the steps of the process and describe them. Decide who will say what. Don't forget to use sequence words and expressions.

Sequence words and expressions	
First, ... To begin / start, ...	After + clause (*After we did that, ...*)
Second, ... Then, ... Next, ...	Finally, ...
Third, ... After that, ...	In the end, ...
When + clause (*When I finished, ...*)	

C. Work in small groups. Give your presentation with your partner.

D. Take notes on your classmates' presentations. Make sure you write down main points and supporting information or ideas for each process. Did your classmates explain the process using sequence words and expressions?

E. Exchange notes with your classmates. With your partner, look at your classmates' notes on your presentation. Discuss these questions.

- Are all of your steps for the process in the notes?

- Were there any parts of the process that were unclear?

- How could you improve your presentation?

Self-Assessment		
Yes	**No**	
☐	☐	I was able to understand and take notes on presentations.
☐	☐	I can use sequence words to describe a process.
☐	☐	I can listen for main and supporting ideas.
☐	☐	I can understand common reductions in speech.
☐	☐	I can correctly use the target vocabulary words from the unit.

Discussion Questions

With a partner or in a small group, discuss the following questions.

1. Is there something you would like to learn how to make? What is it?

2. Do you watch any television programs about people making things? Which ones?

3. When you learn a process for doing something, do you learn better by watching someone else, listening to an explanation, or reading instructions?

The Academic Word List

Words targeted in Level Intro are bold.

Word	Sublist	Location
🔑 abandon	8	L2, U4
abstract	6	L3, U3
academy	5	L2, U10
🔑 **access**	**4**	**L0, U5**
accommodate	9	L3, U6
🔑 accompany	8	L4, U2
accumulate	8	L3, U4
🔑 **accurate**	**6**	**L0, U2**
🔑 **achieve**	**2**	**L0, U4**
🔑 **acknowledge**	**6**	**L0, U7**
🔑 acquire	2	L3, U9
🔑 adapt	7	L3, U7
🔑 adequate	4	L3, U9
adjacent	10	L4, U4
🔑 adjust	5	L4, U4
administrate	2	L4, U8
🔑 **adult**	**7**	**L0, U10**
advocate	7	L4, U3
🔑 affect	2	L1, U1
aggregate	6	L4, U6
🔑 **aid**	**7**	**L0, U5**
albeit	10	L4, U3
allocate	6	L3, U6
🔑 alter	5	L2, U6
🔑 alternative	3	L1, U1
ambiguous	8	L4, U7
amend	5	L4, U7
analogy	9	L4, U1
🔑 analyze	1	L1, U3
🔑 annual	4	L1, U9
🔑 anticipate	9	L2, U8
apparent	4	L2, U4
append	8	L4, U10
🔑 **appreciate**	**8**	**L0, U9**
🔑 approach	1	L1, U1
🔑 appropriate	2	L3, U5
🔑 approximate	4	L2, U7
arbitrary	8	L4, U7
🔑 area	1	L3, U7
🔑 aspect	2	L2, U7
assemble	10	L3, U1
assess	1	L2, U8
assign	6	L3, U5
🔑 **assist**	**2**	**L0, U2**
🔑 assume	1	L3, U1
🔑 assure	9	L4, U8
🔑 **attach**	**6**	**L0, U10**

Word	Sublist	Location
attain	9	L3, U5
🔑 attitude	4	L2, U4
attribute	4	L3, U8
🔑 **author**	**6**	**L0, U1**
🔑 authority	1	L2, U2
automate	8	L2, U1
🔑 **available**	**1**	**L0, U8**
🔑 aware	5	L1, U1
🔑 behalf	9	L4, U9
🔑 benefit	1	L1, U2
bias	8	L4, U3
🔑 bond	6	L4, U9
🔑 brief	6	L2, U9
bulk	9	L3, U1
🔑 capable	6	L3, U5
🔑 capacity	5	L3, U2
🔑 category	2	L2, U4
🔑 cease	9	L2, U2
🔑 challenge	5	L1, U6
🔑 channel	7	L4, U5
🔑 **chapter**	**2**	**L0, U2**
🔑 **chart**	**8**	**L0, U2**
🔑 chemical	7	L2, U6
🔑 circumstance	3	L4, U2
cite	6	L4, U4
🔑 civil	4	L3, U2
clarify	8	L3, U7
🔑 classic	7	L3, U6
clause	5	L4, U8
🔑 **code**	**4**	**L0, U5**
coherent	9	L4, U7
coincide	9	L4, U10
🔑 collapse	10	L3, U9
🔑 colleague	10	L1, U5
commence	9	L2, U4
🔑 comment	3	L1, U4
🔑 commission	2	L3, U2
🔑 commit	4	L2, U1
commodity	8	L4, U4
🔑 communicate	4	L1, U3
🔑 community	2	L1, U4
compatible	9	L2, U4
compensate	3	L4, U8
compile	10	L4, U9
complement	8	L4, U8

🔑 Oxford 3000™ words

Word	Sublist	Location
🔑 complex	2	L2, U1
🔑 component	3	L3, U1
compound	5	L3, U10
comprehensive	7	L2, U6
comprise	7	L3, U7
compute	2	L1, U8
conceive	10	L4, U7
🔑 concentrate	4	L1, U5
🔑 concept	1	L3, U10
🔑 **conclude**	**2**	**L0, U6**
concurrent	9	L4, U10
🔑 conduct	2	L1, U4
confer	4	L4, U8
confine	9	L4, U8
🔑 confirm	7	L1, U8
🔑 conflict	5	L1, U7
conform	8	L3, U6
consent	3	L3, U3
consequent	2	L4, U2
🔑 considerable	3	L4, U1
🔑 consist	1	L1, U9
🔑 constant	3	L1, U8
constitute	1	L4, U5
constrain	3	L4, U6
🔑 construct	2	L3, U1
🔑 consult	5	L2, U8
consume	2	L2, U6
🔑 contact	5	L1, U4
🔑 contemporary	8	L4, U6
🔑 context	1	L2, U4
🔑 contract	1	L3, U4
contradict	8	L2, U4
contrary	7	L3, U1
🔑 contrast	4	L3, U2
🔑 contribute	3	L1, U9
controversy	9	L2, U9
convene	3	L4, U1
converse	9	L2, U2
🔑 convert	7	L3, U3
🔑 convince	10	L1, U5
cooperate	6	L3, U6
coordinate	3	L2, U2
🔑 core	3	L4, U10
corporate	3	L1, U7
correspond	3	L2, U10
🔑 **couple**	**7**	**L0, U4**
🔑 create	1	L3, U7
🔑 credit	2	L2, U7
🔑 criteria	3	L3, U2
🔑 crucial	8	L3, U7
🔑 **culture**	**2**	**L0, U10**

Word	Sublist	Location
currency	8	L2, U3
🔑 cycle	4	L3, U5
🔑 **data**	**1**	**L0, U4**
🔑 debate	4	L3, U5
🔑 decade	7	L1, U9
🔑 decline	5	L1, U9
deduce	3	L4, U10
🔑 **define**	**1**	**L0, U8**
🔑 definite	7	L4, U8
🔑 demonstrate	3	L1, U2
denote	8	L4, U10
🔑 deny	7	L1, U8
🔑 **depress**	**10**	**L0, U8**
🔑 derive	1	L4, U8
🔑 **design**	**2**	**L0, U10**
🔑 despite	4	L3, U6
detect	8	L2, U3
deviate	8	L4, U10
🔑 **device**	**9**	**L0, U2**
🔑 devote	9	L2, U3
differentiate	7	L3, U6
dimension	4	L4, U9
diminish	9	L2, U8
discrete	5	L4, U2
discriminate	6	L4, U5
displace	8	L3, U10
🔑 **display**	**6**	**L0, U8**
dispose	7	L4, U1
distinct	2	L4, U2
distort	9	L4, U5
🔑 distribute	1	L1, U9
diverse	6	L3, U2
🔑 **document**	**3**	**L0, U4**
domain	6	L4, U6
🔑 domestic	4	L2, U5
🔑 dominate	3	L3, U7
🔑 **draft**	**5**	**L0, U10**
🔑 drama	8	L2, U9
duration	9	L2, U3
dynamic	7	L3, U3
🔑 economy	1	L2, U8
edit	6	L1, U7
🔑 element	2	L3, U1
🔑 eliminate	7	L1, U6
🔑 emerge	4	L3, U5
🔑 emphasis	3	L1, U5
empirical	7	L4, U4
🔑 enable	5	L2, U1
🔑 encounter	10	L1, U8

🔑 Oxford 3000™ words

Word	Sublist	Location
🔑 **energy**	**5**	**L0, U9**
enforce	5	L4, U1
enhance	6	L3, U2
🔑 **enormous**	**10**	**L0, U7**
🔑 ensure	3	L4, U1
entity	5	L4, U8
🔑 environment	1	L1, U1
equate	2	L3, U10
equip	7	L2, U1
🔑 equivalent	5	L1, U7
erode	9	L4, U2
🔑 **error**	**4**	**L0, U2**
🔑 establish	1	L2, U5
🔑 estate	6	L4, U8
🔑 estimate	1	L2, U5
ethic	9	L3, U4
🔑 ethnic	4	L3, U9
evaluate	2	L1, U8
eventual	8	L3, U2
evident	1	L2, U8
evolve	5	L2, U2
exceed	6	L1, U10
🔑 exclude	3	L3, U8
🔑 exhibit	8	L2, U3
🔑 **expand**	**5**	**L0, U5**
🔑 **expert**	**6**	**L0, U3**
explicit	6	L4, U3
exploit	8	L4, U9
🔑 export	1	L4, U6
🔑 expose	5	L4, U1
external	5	L2, U1
extract	7	L3, U1
facilitate	5	L3, U6
🔑 factor	1	L3, U1
🔑 **feature**	**2**	**L0, U2**
🔑 federal	6	L4, U4
🔑 **fee**	**6**	**L0, U5**
🔑 **file**	**7**	**L0, U5**
🔑 **final**	**2**	**L0, U1**
🔑 finance	1	L3, U6
finite	7	L4, U9
flexible	6	L1, U10
fluctuate	8	L4, U10
🔑 **focus**	**2**	**L0, U6**
format	9	L2, U8
🔑 formula	1	L3, U5
forthcoming	10	L4, U10
🔑 **found**	**9**	**L0, U7**
🔑 foundation	7	L1, U9
framework	3	L4, U6

Word	Sublist	Location
🔑 function	1	L3, U3
🔑 fund	3	L2, U5
🔑 fundamental	5	L1, U8
furthermore	6	L3, U4
gender	6	L3, U8
🔑 generate	5	L1, U5
🔑 generation	5	L2, U10
globe	7	L2, U5
🔑 **goal**	**4**	**L0, U7**
🔑 **grade**	**7**	**L0, U3**
🔑 grant	4	L3, U9
🔑 guarantee	7	L1, U7
guideline	8	L1, U6
hence	4	L3, U6
hierarchy	7	L4, U6
🔑 **highlight**	**8**	**L0, U7**
hypothesis	4	L3, U4
identical	7	L3, U3
🔑 identify	1	L1, U3
ideology	7	L4, U3
ignorance	6	L2, U9
🔑 **illustrate**	**3**	**L0, U1**
🔑 image	5	L1, U3
immigrate	3	L4, U7
🔑 impact	2	L2, U9
implement	4	L4, U2
implicate	4	L4, U3
implicit	8	L4, U3
🔑 imply	3	L3, U8
🔑 impose	4	L3, U10
incentive	6	L4, U2
incidence	6	L3, U4
incline	10	L4, U4
🔑 **income**	**1**	**L0, U4**
incorporate	6	L4, U9
🔑 index	6	L4, U9
🔑 indicate	1	L2, U10
🔑 **individual**	**1**	**L0, U1**
induce	8	L4, U1
🔑 inevitable	8	L3, U2
infer	7	L4, U3
infrastructure	8	L4, U1
inherent	9	L4, U7
inhibit	6	L4, U2
🔑 **initial**	**3**	**L0, U3**
initiate	6	L3, U8
🔑 injure	2	L4, U9
innovate	7	L3, U1

🔑 Oxford 3000™ words

Word	Sublist	Location
input	6	L2, U5
insert	7	L2, U7
insight	9	L3, U4
inspect	8	L4, U9
🔑 instance	3	L3, U3
🔑 institute	2	L1, U6
instruct	6	L1, U6
integral	9	L4, U6
integrate	4	L4, U6
integrity	10	L2, U1
🔑 **intelligence**	**6**	**L0, U10**
🔑 intense	8	L3, U7
interact	3	L2, U3
intermediate	9	L2, U5
🔑 internal	4	L1, U10
interpret	1	L3, U10
🔑 interval	6	L3, U10
intervene	7	L3, U6
intrinsic	10	L4, U7
🔑 invest	2	L3, U2
🔑 investigate	4	L2, U9
invoke	10	L4, U5
🔑 involve	1	L3, U7
isolate	7	L3, U2
🔑 **issue**	**1**	**L0, U3**
🔑 **item**	**2**	**L0, U6**
🔑 **job**	**4**	**L0, U10**
journal	2	L1, U10
🔑 justify	3	L4, U2
🔑 **label**	**4**	**L0, U1**
🔑 labor	1	L2, U4
🔑 layer	3	L3, U3
🔑 **lecture**	**6**	**L0, U6**
🔑 legal	1	L1, U2
legislate	1	L4, U1
levy	10	L4, U3
🔑 liberal	5	L4, U3
🔑 license	5	L3, U8
likewise	10	L3, U4
🔑 **link**	**3**	**L0, U4**
🔑 locate	3	L1, U4
🔑 logic	5	L3, U5
🔑 maintain	2	L1, U10
🔑 major	1	L3, U7
manipulate	8	L4, U10
manual	9	L3, U10
margin	5	L2, U3
mature	9	L2, U8

Word	Sublist	Location
maximize	3	L1, U9
mechanism	4	L3, U3
🔑 **media**	**7**	**L0, U8**
mediate	9	L4, U10
🔑 medical	5	L1, U2
🔑 medium	9	L1, U10
🔑 mental	5	L2, U6
🔑 method	1	L1, U2
migrate	6	L4, U1
🔑 military	9	L2, U3
minimal	9	L1, U9
minimize	8	L3, U1
🔑 minimum	6	L1, U10
🔑 ministry	6	L4, U6
🔑 **minor**	**3**	**L0, U7**
mode	7	L4, U5
modify	5	L1, U6
🔑 monitor	5	L3, U4
motive	6	L2, U7
mutual	9	L2, U2
negate	3	L4, U4
🔑 network	5	L2, U2
neutral	6	L2, U5
🔑 nevertheless	6	L3, U5
nonetheless	10	L4, U5
norm	9	L4, U7
🔑 **normal**	**2**	**L0, U6**
🔑 notion	5	L3, U5
notwithstanding	10	L4, U6
🔑 nuclear	8	L3, U9
🔑 **objective**	**5**	**L0, U4**
🔑 obtain	2	L3, U4
🔑 obvious	4	L1, U7
🔑 occupy	4	L4, U8
🔑 occur	1	L2, U10
🔑 odd	10	L1, U8
offset	8	L4, U9
ongoing	10	L2, U7
🔑 option	4	L1, U10
orient	5	L4, U4
outcome	3	L2, U7
🔑 output	4	L2, U5
🔑 overall	4	L2, U9
overlap	9	L2, U4
🔑 overseas	6	L2, U3
🔑 panel	10	L4, U5
paradigm	7	L4, U2
paragraph	8	L1, U7

🔑 Oxford 3000™ words

Word	Sublist	Location	Word	Sublist	Location
⚷ parallel	4	L4, U3	radical	8	L4, U5
parameter	4	L3, U4	random	8	L2, U5
⚷ participate	2	L1, U2	⚷ range	2	L2, U10
⚷ **partner**	**3**	**L0, U3**	ratio	5	L3, U10
passive	9	L3, U10	rational	6	L3, U9
perceive	2	L3, U7	⚷ react	3	L1, U3
⚷ percent	1	L1, U3	⚷ recover	6	L2, U1
⚷ period	1	L3, U3	refine	9	L3, U5
persist	10	L3, U4	regime	4	L3, U9
⚷ perspective	5	L2, U10	⚷ region	2	L2, U2
⚷ phase	4	L2, U10	⚷ register	3	L3, U8
phenomenon	7	L4, U4	regulate	2	L2, U2
⚷ philosophy	3	L3, U8	reinforce	8	L3, U4
⚷ **physical**	**3**	**L0, U1**	⚷ reject	5	L1, U10
⚷ **plus**	**8**	**L0, U6**	⚷ **relax**	**9**	**L0, U6**
⚷ policy	1	L2, U9	⚷ release	7	L2, U5
portion	9	L2, U6	⚷ relevant	2	L3, U8
⚷ pose	10	L4, U4	reluctant	10	L2, U3
⚷ **positive**	**2**	**L0, U7**	⚷ rely	3	L2, U9
⚷ potential	2	L2, U10	⚷ **remove**	**3**	**L0, U9**
practitioner	8	L4, U1	⚷ **require**	**1**	**L0, U10**
precede	6	L3, U9	⚷ **research**	**1**	**L0, U3**
⚷ precise	5	L3, U3	reside	2	L4, U3
⚷ **predict**	**4**	**L0, U9**	⚷ resolve	4	L2, U4
predominant	8	L4, U5	⚷ **resource**	**2**	**L0, U3**
preliminary	9	L2, U2	⚷ respond	1	L1, U4
presume	6	L4, U7	⚷ restore	8	L2, U10
⚷ **previous**	**2**	**L0, U9**	restrain	9	L3, U9
⚷ primary	2	L1, U3	⚷ restrict	2	L2, U7
prime	5	L4, U2	⚷ retain	4	L4, U7
⚷ principal	4	L2, U10	⚷ reveal	6	L2, U1
⚷ principle	1	L3, U10	revenue	5	L3, U6
⚷ prior	4	L2, U8	⚷ reverse	7	L3, U9
⚷ priority	7	L2, U6	⚷ revise	8	L1, U7
⚷ proceed	1	L2, U1	⚷ revolution	9	L3, U3
⚷ process	1	L1, U2	rigid	9	L2, U6
⚷ professional	4	L1, U2	⚷ **role**	**1**	**L0, U9**
prohibit	7	L3, U2	⚷ route	9	L3, U9
⚷ project	4	L1, U9			
⚷ promote	4	L4, U7	scenario	9	L2, U7
⚷ proportion	3	L2, U8	⚷ schedule	7	L1, U5
⚷ prospect	8	L4, U6	scheme	3	L3, U2
protocol	9	L4, U9	scope	6	L2, U9
psychology	5	L2, U8	⚷ **section**	**1**	**L0, U9**
⚷ publication	7	L3, U9	⚷ sector	1	L4, U6
⚷ **publish**	**3**	**L0, U1**	⚷ secure	2	L1, U6
⚷ **purchase**	**2**	**L0, U7**	⚷ seek	2	L2, U7
⚷ pursue	5	L4, U4	⚷ select	2	L1, U4
			sequence	3	L1, U6
qualitative	9	L4, U8	⚷ **series**	**4**	**L0, U9**
⚷ quote	7	L1, U7	⚷ sex	3	L4, U4

⚷ Oxford 3000™ words

Word	Sublist	Location
🔑 shift	3	L2, U7
🔑 significant	1	L3, U2
🔑 similar	1	L1, U5
simulate	7	L3, U4
🔑 **site**	**2**	**L0, U5**
so-called	10	L2, U9
sole	7	L4, U10
🔑 somewhat	7	L3, U7
🔑 source	1	L1, U1
🔑 specific	1	L1, U6
specify	3	L1, U8
sphere	9	L4, U6
🔑 stable	5	L3, U10
statistic	4	L3, U8
🔑 **status**	**4**	**L0, U4**
straightforward	10	L3, U6
🔑 strategy	2	L2, U2
🔑 stress	4	L3, U7
🔑 structure	1	L2, U1
🔑 style	5	L2, U2
submit	7	L1, U10
subordinate	9	L4, U3
subsequent	4	L3, U5
subsidy	6	L4, U8
🔑 substitute	5	L2, U3
successor	7	L3, U6
🔑 sufficient	3	L4, U2
🔑 sum	4	L3, U9
🔑 summary	4	L1, U3
supplement	9	L2, U6
🔑 survey	2	L2, U6
🔑 survive	7	L2, U9
suspend	9	L4, U5
sustain	5	L3, U1
🔑 **symbol**	**5**	**L0, U8**
🔑 tape	6	L3, U8
🔑 target	5	L2, U6
🔑 **task**	**3**	**L0, U5**
🔑 **team**	**9**	**L0, U3**
🔑 technical	3	L3, U3
🔑 technique	3	L3, U5
🔑 technology	3	L2, U10
🔑 **temporary**	**9**	**L0, U8**
tense	7	L2, U6
terminate	7	L4, U10
🔑 **text**	**2**	**L0, U1**
🔑 theme	7	L1, U5
🔑 theory	1	L3, U8
thereby	7	L4, U7
thesis	7	L4, U7

Word	Sublist	Location
🔑 **topic**	**7**	**L0, U6**
🔑 trace	6	L4, U5
🔑 **tradition**	**2**	**L0, U2**
🔑 transfer	2	L1, U6
🔑 transform	6	L3, U1
transit	5	L2, U8
transmit	7	L4, U1
🔑 transport	6	L1, U1
🔑 trend	5	L1, U4
trigger	9	L4, U1
🔑 ultimate	7	L3, U8
undergo	10	L4, U9
underlie	6	L4, U5
undertake	4	L4, U2
🔑 uniform	7	L2, U4
unify	9	L2, U5
🔑 unique	7	L3, U10
utilize	6	L3, U1
🔑 valid	3	L3, U8
🔑 vary	1	L2, U1
🔑 vehicle	7	L1, U1
🔑 version	5	L1, U7
🔑 via	7	L4, U4
violate	9	L4, U3
virtual	8	L3, U3
🔑 visible	7	L2, U6
🔑 **vision**	**9**	**L0, U8**
visual	8	L3, U7
🔑 volume	3	L1, U8
voluntary	7	L3, U10
welfare	5	L4, U9
🔑 whereas	5	L4, U5
whereby	10	L4, U10
widespread	7	L2, U3

🔑 Oxford 3000™ words